# Longing for the Holy

## Spirituality for Everyday Life

Based on Selected Insights of

Ronald Rolheiser, O.M.I.

RENEW International

NIHIL OBSTAT
Reverend Lawrence E. Frizzell, D.Phil.
Censor Librorum

IMPRIMATUR
Most Reverend John J. Myers, J.C.D., D.D.
Archbishop of Newark

Cover design by Robert B. Kelly
Text design by James F. Brisson
Text illustration by Marion C. Honors, C.S.J.

ISBN  1-930978-90-1

**RENEW International**
1232 George Street
Plainfield, NJ 07062-1717
To order, call 1-888-433-3221
www.renewintl.org

Printed and bound in the United States of America

# Contents

With Gratitude  v

Presenting RENEW International  vii

Foreword  ix

Introduction  1

A Prayer of Spiritual Longing  9

SESSION 1
Spirituality:
Channeling Our Life-Giving Energy  11

SESSION 2
The Challenge of Our Culture  21

SESSION 3
Spirituality in a Christian Context:
Love of God and Neighbor  31

SESSION 4
Spirituality in a Christian Context:
A Heart for God and Each Other  41

SESSION 5
Incarnation:
Christ in Us  53

# CONTENTS

SESSION 6

## The Paschal Mystery:
The Offer of New Life   65

SESSION 7

## In My House There Are Many Rooms:
Being a Part of Church Community   79

SESSION 8

## Eucharist:
God's Gift and Our Response   91

SESSION 9

## Walk Justly   103

SESSION 10

## Loving Well:
Spirituality and Sexuality   117

SESSION 11

## Living the Life   129

SESSION 12

## Being a Mystic in Everyday Life:
Finding God in All Things   143

Music Appendix   157

Addresses of Publishers of Music Resources   160

Acknowledgments   161

# With Gratitude

WE ARE DEEPLY GRATEFUL to Reverend Ronald Rolheiser, O.M.I., for meeting with our staff members and graciously permitting us to use selections from his spiritual insights in this endeavor. Without his giftedness and support, *Longing for the Holy* would not have come to fruition.

We are also grateful to the authors and publishers who granted permission for material under their copyright to be quoted in this book. All of these uses are clearly detailed on pages 161-162.

We acknowledge and thank the many diocesan and parish staff members whose insights and direct feedback contributed greatly to this work. We are also grateful to the hundreds of small Christian community participants who read and piloted these sessions and who offered enthusiastic responses and valuable ideas.

# Presenting
# RENEW International

*L*ONGING FOR THE HOLY: Spirituality for Everyday Life is a 12-session process of spiritual and pastoral renewal developed by RENEW International. The *Longing for the Holy* process is one of the most recent among those that RENEW offers.

The RENEW process, both parish-based and diocesan-wide, was first developed and implemented in the Archdiocese of Newark, New Jersey. Its success there led other dioceses, in the United States, and in other countries, to bring RENEW to their people and parish communities. In the three decades since its vibrant beginnings, RENEW International has touched the lives of 25 million people in over 150 dioceses in the United States and 23 countries throughout the world.

RENEW International has grown organically from its original single RENEW process. Materials and training have been inculturated and made available in over 40 languages. We have added specific pastoral outreach to campuses, and to young adults in their 20s and 30s. We have incorporated prison ministry, and provided resources for the visually impaired.

The very core of all of these processes remains the same: to help people become better hearers and doers of the Word of God. We do this by encouraging and supporting the formation of small communities who gather prayerfully to reflect on and share the Word of God, to make better connections between faith and life, and to live their faith more concretely in family, work, and community life.

As a not-for-profit organization, our pastoral outreach is sustained in part from the sales of our publications and resources, and the stipends we receive for the services provided to parishes and dioceses. However, our priority is always to serve all parishes who desire to renew their faith and build the Church, regardless of their economic situation. We have been able to fulfill this mission not only in the inner city and rural areas in the United States, but also in the developing world, especially Latin America and Africa, thanks to donations and charitable funding.

As you meet in your small group, we invite you to take a few moments to imagine the great invisible network of others, here in the United States and on the other continents. They gather, as you do, in small Christian communities, around the Word of God present in the Scripture, striving to hear and act upon that Word. Keep them in your prayer: a prayer of thanksgiving for the many graces we have experienced; a prayer that the Spirit will guide all of us as we strive to respond to our "longing for the holy."

✠ ✠ ✠

# RENEW International's
# Mission Statement

RENEW International
fosters spiritual renewal in the Catholic tradition
by empowering individuals and communities
to encounter God in everyday life,
deepen and share faith,
and connect faith with action.

✠ ✠ ✠

# Foreword

ONE SIZE DOESN'T FIT ALL! That isn't just true of clothing; it's true, also, of spirituality and discipleship.

The invitations that Jesus gives us to ultimately be perfect as God is perfect grow deeper and deeper as we mature in life. What discipleship asks of us in mid-life or when we are facing death is not the same as what it asks of us in our twenties, when we are still trying to find ourselves. For example, during the first half of life, success can teach us some valuable lessons. During the second half of life, success still feels good and we yearn for it, but it has much less to teach us and can, in fact, be a hindrance to real growth. The different seasons in our lives call for a different depth in terms of discipleship.

When we look at the Gospels, as well as at the classical Christian mystics, we see that discipleship, following of Christ, has three basic levels. We might name them: *Essential Discipleship, Generative Discipleship*, and *Radical Discipleship*.

Simply put: *Essential Discipleship* is that part of life where we are *trying to get our lives together; Generative Discipleship* is that part of life when we are *trying to give our lives away;* and *Radical Discipleship* is that part of life where we are *trying to give our deaths away.*

What does that mean?

We are born into a home and we get to live there until we reach puberty. Puberty is designed by God and by nature to drive us out of our homes into the world where we need to create our own homes. This is the first real part of our own spiritual journey and sometimes it takes many years before we find our way back home again, to a place where we have found a life partner, a vocation, a job, a meaning, and a home of our own. That is the struggle to come to *Essential Discipleship*. Sometimes, sadly, we never get there.

But once we do get there, the struggle changes. Now it is no longer a question of finding ourselves but of giving our lives away in generosity and service of others—family, church, country, world. The struggle now is to be *generative*, to live lives that make a difference, to find ever deeper ways to give ourselves over. This is what the mystics call *Proficiency*. Ideally we will spend most of the years of our adult lives in this stage, namely, *Generative Discipleship*, trying to give our lives away.

However, as T.S. Eliot says: *Home is where we start from!* Just as we had to leave the home we were first born into, we, too, have to leave this place in our lives, the home we created for ourselves. Nobody exits this planet alive and there comes a time when our spiritual task is not so much that of giving our lives away but that of *giving our deaths away*. Henri Nouwen put it this way: There comes a point in life where the question is no longer: How can I live my life so that I make a difference? How can I live so as to give myself more deeply to others? Rather the question becomes: How can I now live so that when I die my death will be an optimal blessing for my family, the Church, and my community? That is the task of *Radical Discipleship*, something the mystics called "the dark night of the Spirit" and that is what Jesus illustrates for us when he undergoes his passion and death.

*The Holy Longing* is a book that deals mainly with the first two levels: *Essential* and *Generative Discipleship*. Its intent is to try to offer guidance in terms of the struggle to get our lives together and to give them away in love and service.

And underneath this basic intent, there is a secondary one: When Eric Major (formerly the Religious Editor at Doubleday) asked me to write *The Holy Longing*, he worded his request this way: "Write a book that I can give to my adult children that will explain to them why I still believe in God and go to church — and that I can read myself on those days when I'm not so sure any more why I believe in God and go to church!" He knew what was needed. We live in a time of great freedom, great pluralism, and great confusion. We need someone to help us name the essentials. *The Holy Longing* tries to do that and *Longing for the Holy* is a huge help in highlighting those essentials and making suggestions as to how we might integrate them more into our lives.

May this faith-sharing resource help you outstrip me in understanding, generosity, and discipleship!

Ronald Rolheiser, O.M.I.
Oblate School of Theology
San Antonio, Texas
April 28, 2007

# Longing
## for the
# Holy

# Introduction

EVERYONE IS SPIRITUAL. Whether or not we are fully conscious of it, our spirits long to be united with a greater good, a deeper meaning, a wider love than we may experience in our everyday lives. We long for intimacy, to be connected, to belong, to be part of something or someone bigger than ourselves. We long to experience the connection to all that is within our universe and with the Creator who fashioned us and that universe. Yet, time seems to slip from our grasp, our days are filled with everyday tasks, and cultural values often draw us away from the most essential meaning of life—living in the presence of God and responding to the needs of God's people.

In *Longing for the Holy*, we explore the implications of the central mysteries of faith—the Incarnation, Eucharist, and the Paschal Mystery—for spirituality. We attend to the cultural challenges that keep us from realizing our true desire and we consider the important themes of church community, justice, sexuality, the practices of the spiritual life, and being a mystic of the everyday. *Longing for the Holy* respects our traditional Catholic roots yet offers a strong but flexible approach to spirituality. And because God created each of us uniquely, each one's approach to spirituality, to prayer, and to action will also be unique.

We owe a debt of gratitude to Father Ronald Rolheiser, OMI, a member of the Oblates of Mary Immaculate, whose classic works on spirituality, *The Holy Longing* and *The Shattered Lantern,* inspired this work. In these books, Fr. Rolheiser explores the spiritual implications of the Christian story for our spiritual development. Spirituality, Rolheiser suggests, is *what we do with our desire.* It concerns the way we channel the deep longing that is at the core of our beings. We all have such desire. The problem is we don't always know what to do with it. Much of the anguish of human existence is caused by human failure to appropriately identify and discipline that desire. As we progress in *Longing for the Holy,* we will see what components Rolheiser sees as necessary for a genuinely Christian spirituality that takes the love story of the triune God and humanity seriously.

We hope these sessions will help enrich our sense of the presence of God in our lives—in the personal, familial, work, civic, religious, and cultural arenas—and assist us in responding to God's presence with deep faith, expanding love, and a renewed commitment to justice.

# Before You Begin

Any practice of our faith, any prayer, worship, activity, or study, asks of us a certain attentiveness. We say we know God's love surrounds us at every moment of our lives, but we are busy people. We might find it hard to take the time to remember God's goodness to us in the past. We might find it difficult to sense God's presence with us in the present. In this, we are no different from generations of Christians before us. They knew, as we know, that some simple, straightforward help is necessary to become more attentive to our gracious and good God.

Like them, whenever we gather together, we prepare ourselves to become attentive. Part of this preparation is reading and reflecting on the upcoming session before the group gathers. So, each time you gather as a group to pray through the exercises in *Longing for the Holy*, you will engage in a little preparatory ritual that will help you to open your hearts and minds to God's voice, as God will speak to you.

# First Gathering

At the first meeting when your group is seated, you will be invited to briefly introduce yourself. The leader can set the pace by first introducing herself or himself.

# Sharing

**"How am I right now?" or
"What good news would I like to share?"**

You will be invited to share your response to one of the following questions, "How am I right now?" or "What good news would I like to share?" This should be a very brief but honest assessment of where you find yourself. "I'm tired; I've been taking care of my mother who's been having chemotherapy." Or, "I am so happy; our son has really improved his grades this semester." Or, "I'm just glad to be here; we've been working a lot of over-time at the office." There will be time to go into details infor-mally later. It is enough to be mindful that God finds us where we *are* not where we think we *ought* to be.

## Sharing the Good News

After the first session, you will have a chance to share with oth-ers how you incorporated the message of each session into your daily lives or how the Word of God challenged you into action for the week ahead.

## Lifting Our Hearts ...

### ... in Song

Next, as part of your becoming attentive, you will be invited to listen to a piece of music or to sing a song. You may use the songs suggested in *Longing for the Holy* or you may choose music that has particular meaning for your group. Music allows us to become aware of the often-ignored parts of ourselves that can sense God's presence.

### ... in the Quiet

In order to enter more deeply into the presence of God, you will be invited to quiet yourself, to, as it were, shake the dust of the day off your feet. Taking a few deep breaths and consciously let-ting go of any tension in your body may help to do this. Since the earliest days, the Christian community has valued silence not simply as the restful absence of sound, but as an important practice, as a way that we learn to really listen—to God, to each other, to our own hearts.

## ... in the Word

Then, one of your group (choose a different person each session) will read aloud a passage from Scripture. Please read slowly. Read with the same attention and joy that you would give to a letter that has come from a family member or a beloved. The Scriptures are God's love letters to us. After the reading, pause for a time of silence to ponder the Word of God. Let God's Word speak to your heart.

## ... in Prayer

The group will conclude this section by offering together a closing prayer, opening hearts to communion with God. Keep in mind that the faith sharing that follows is also prayer, and is meant to help us grow in our union with Christ.

# Our Companion on the Journey

Each of the reflections contains a quote from a wise Christian who has gone before us. These holy ones are a "cloud of witnesses" (Hebrews 12:1) who show us the many faces of holiness, the many ways Christ is visible in the world. The sense of being surrounded by a "cloud of witnesses"—the communion of saints—is a strong belief in our Catholic tradition. Saints are not plaster of Paris statues or generic holy people. Rather, they are, like us, unique individuals who struggled, each with his or her own gifts and weaknesses, to embody the Christ life in a different moment and place in history. They are companions who can encourage us to live fully in Christ in our own era and circumstances. May these holy ones be companions for you as you respond—in your own way—to that call.

## Encountering Wisdom for Life

Take some time to read and review the reflection you already prepared at home. This may be done either aloud or silently. When you are finished, pause to consider what you have read. You may want to reflect more on the lines or phrases you have underlined.

## Sharing Our Faith

You will then begin your sharing about the questions in the session of *Longing for the Holy*. (You may have jotted down some of your responses previously.) One person may read the question aloud, and then leave time for others to respond. Please listen to each other with reverence, adhering to principles of confidentiality. This is the place to support and encourage one another, not make judgments about each other's spiritual life or ideas. Each of us is a beloved child of God. None of us is flawless. For this brief time, we listen to one another with God's compassionate love. Sharing yourself and being open to the sharing of others is a great gift each member of the group can offer.

## Living the Good News

You will be invited to choose an action that emerges from the Word of God, the specific context of your life, and/or from your sharing. This should be your primary consideration. When choosing an individual action, determine what you will do and share it with the group. When choosing a group action, determine who will take responsibility for different aspects of the action. Suggested actions are listed.

## Closing Prayer

When you have finished sharing your thoughts, you will pray together. Intercessory prayers—prayer for the concerns that weigh on your hearts—are appropriate, as are prayers of thanksgiving and praise.

## Looking Ahead

Just a reminder—Prepare at home for the following meeting by prayerfully reading and reflecting on the next session before you meet again.

## Informal Gathering

Finally, if you plan to have some informal gathering, perhaps with snacks, this is the time to do that and a nice way to close your time together.

So, your time together, approximately two hours, would look something like this:

| | | |
|---|---|---|
| **1.** **Sharing\*** <br> **"How am I feeling right now?" or** <br> **"What good news would I like to share?"** | | **20 min.** |
| **2.** **Lifting Our Hearts …** <br> **… in Song** <br> **… in the Quiet** <br> **… in the Word** <br> **… in Prayer** | | **20 min.** |
| **3.** **Our Companion on the Journey** | | **5 min.** |
| **4.** **Encountering Wisdom for Life** | | **10 min.** |
| **5.** **Sharing Our Faith** | | **30 min.** |
| **6.** **Living the Good News** | | **10 min.** |
| **7.** **Closing Prayer/Looking Ahead** | | **10 min.** |
| **8.** **Informal Gathering** | | **15 min.** |

\*In Session 1, during the time for Sharing, briefly introduce yourself. You will begin Sharing the Good News during Session 2.

Becoming accustomed to a simple pattern such as this frees us from always having to figure out what comes next. It allows us to simply sink into the deeper parts of ourselves and listen together with true attentiveness to God's gracious stirrings in our lives.

## A Note for Small Community Leaders

Two songs are suggested for each session. The first is contained on the *Longing for the Holy* music CD. The second named song may be more familiar and can most likely be found in parish hymnals or missalettes.

# A Prayer of Spiritual Longing

Loving God and Father, we long for you.
We long for deeper meaning in our lives,
for a wider love than we now experience.
We yearn to know we belong
and are connected to you and all creation.

Yet time seems to slip from our grasp,
our days filled with the duties of life.
Often we do not recognize your presence
that calls us to respond to the needs of your people.

Help us to live more consciously
and joyfully in your presence,
to channel the longing at the core of our being
with deep faith, expanding hope,
and a renewed commitment to right relationships.

May we embody the Christ life
in this our moment and place in history.
May the communion of saints surround us
and companion us on our journey.

May your Holy Spirit empower us to be holy
for the good of the world
and for your honor and glory.

We ask this through the risen Christ,
our brother and friend. Amen.

# Spirituality
## Channeling Our Life-Giving Energy

## Sharing

*Briefly share on one of the following questions:*

"How am I right now?" or
"What good news would I like to share?"

## Lifting Our Hearts ...

### ... in Song

*Play or sing one of the following or another song of your choice:*

"Gathered in the Love of Christ"
"Your Love Is Finer Than Life"

### ... in the Quiet

*Pause for a few moments of silence and enter more deeply into the presence of God.*

### ... in the Word

*Read aloud* Psalm 33:6-9, 13-15, 20-22.

*Take a few minutes to ponder a word, a phrase, a question,
or a feeling that rises up in you. Reflect on this quietly;
then share it aloud.*

*(Even if no one wishes to reflect aloud, permit sufficient time
for silent reflection.)*

### ... in Prayer

*Conclude with this prayer spoken together:*

> Gracious and loving God,
> the world around us astonishes us with its beauty.
> Into this remarkable world you have placed us,
> your sons, your daughters,
> created in your very image.
> May we always remember who we are
> and to whom we truly belong.
> Amen.

## Our Companion on the Journey

# St. Augustine

"Our hearts are restless until they rest in you."

St. Augustine (4th-5th centuries, North Africa)

A S A YOUNG MAN, Augustine lived very intensely. He had a mistress and an illegitimate son, explored many different philosophies, and tried to make his mark in the world by becoming a dazzling teacher of rhetoric. His mother, Monica, was a Christian and prayed that her son might follow her in that faith. Eventually, after a painful interior struggle and thanks to the counseling and instruction of Ambrose, Bishop of Milan, Augustine converted. In time, he became Bishop of Hippo in North Africa. His many sermons and writings profoundly influenced the course of western theology. His autobiographical book, *The Confessions*, is a classic account of the human struggle involved in channeling vital energies.

## Encountering Wisdom for Life

GO INTO ANY BOOKSTORE today. Lining the shelves of at least one section you will find all sorts of books grouped under the title "Spirituality." Self-help, pop-psychology, health and wellness, esoteric practices are all mixed in with the sacred texts and classic writings of the religions of the world. What, we wonder, *is* spirituality? Or perhaps we wonder: What does Christianity have to do with all this? Fr. Ronald Rolheiser, a Canadian Oblate of Mary Immaculate and author of *The Holy Longing* and *The Shattered Lantern*, can give us some insight. He helps us to explore the question, "What is spirituality?" and the allied questions, for example, "What prevents me from living a deeper spiritual life?"

Rolheiser begins by prompting us to pay attention to the deepest currents of our lives. In each human being, he suggests, there is an energy, a life force that is most often experienced as desire or longing. We long for many things, we feel restless, we seem compelled out of ourselves toward something *more*.

Some ancient Greeks used to say that we are fired into life with a sort of madness that comes from the gods and that this divinely endowed energy is the root of all love, hate, creativity, joy, and sorrow. Rolheiser suggests something similar. Each of us has this deep, driving desire, this longing for *more*.

This energy is so powerful that it can, if we are not mindful, overpower us. Our fiery life force needs to be channeled to be life-giving, not life-consuming.

There are some general observations that can be made about what we do with our desire. A healthy spirituality is one that, in Rolheiser's eyes, does two things: it keeps us energized and it keeps us glued together. In other words, a healthy spirituality gives us zest and hope; it allows us to experience life as beautiful and worth living. It works against the cynicism, despair, and bitterness that can paralyze us. A healthy spirituality is also integrative; it gives us a sense of coherence and order, a sense of who we are, where we are going, and how life is full of meaning.

The task is to balance these two sometimes-conflicting dynamics: the creative, chaotic dynamic that energizes us must be balanced with the ordered, disciplined dynamic of our life. Too much chaos and you die of dissipation; too much order and you die of suffocation. A healthy spirituality is discovered in balance between the two.

Rolheiser offers us the examples of three women who have been our contemporaries to illustrate his point. Each of these had a different relationship to the creative longing at the root of her being. The three may surprise you. They are Mother Teresa of Calcutta, the simple yet powerful religious sister who laid her life down for those who were poor, founder of the Missionaries of Charity; Janis Joplin, the rock and blues singer of the sixties; and Princess Diana, the late mother of Princes William and Harry of England. Each woman had her own very powerful share of fiery desire. But each directed that desire differently. It was disciplined either in life-giving or in life-consuming ways, or in an uneasy combination of the two. It is easy for us to associate Mother Teresa with a vibrant spirituality. She helped the dying poor. But she was also a woman who had disciplined and channeled her powerful desire into a life that was integrated and rooted in a vision larger than her own self-interest. She was able to found a worldwide network of houses for the dying precisely because of her ability to integrate all her deep, fiery energy into the work to which she felt God had called her.

Few would compare Mother Teresa with rock icon, Janis Joplin. Yet both were women with exceptional fire, creativity, and rare energy. Janis Joplin's energy went out in many directions, not all of them life giving. Her rare talent of songwriting was a gift, but frenetic activity, dissipation, and uncontrolled sexual activity led to her death, from a drug overdose, at the age of twenty-seven. Instead of being an integrating force in her life, Joplin's vital desires were undisciplined and eventually consumed her.

Princess Diana's life falls between these other two. Like Joplin, she wanted to taste all the sensation that life has to offer. Fame, wealth, love, and excitement: she wanted it all. Yet she also was driven by a deep desire to care for those whose lives were shattered by poverty and bodies maimed by landmines. Sometimes she was able to focus on these life-giving longings; at other times her other desires held her in sway. Perhaps we are more like Princess Diana than like Mother Teresa or Janis Joplin. At times we may swing between what seem like conflicting desires.

So what does this have to do with spirituality? Spirituality, Rolheiser suggests, is *what we do with our desire.* It concerns the way we channel that deep, raging fire that is at the core of our lives. We all have such longing at the core of our beings. The problem is we do not know always what to do with it. Much of the anguish of human existence is caused by human failure, failure to appropriately identify and discipline that desire. Following are a few considerations that can shed some light on how to focus the fire within.

First, sometimes people think that to be spiritual we have to be otherworldly, to avoid human contact for fear of sullying ourselves, or to be always doing "religious" activities. Rolheiser suggests otherwise. He reminds us that the opposite of being spiritual is to have no energy, to have lost all sense of the zest for life. Walling ourselves off from life is not the point of spirituality. Second, sometimes people think there is one spiritual path that everyone must follow. They look to their pious neighbors or an admired priest, teacher, nun, or holy person and think they must be exactly like them. No one can live another's life. Each person is different and the way that each man or woman directs the deep desire raging within will depend on his or her own circumstances, history, and gifts.

Augustine of Hippo, our companion from the tradition for this session, is a case in point. Augustine was a man of great, vital energy, and during much of his early life he was buffeted about by those energies. He was competitive, driven to succeed in his profession, and had intense and complex relationships with a number of women. He was, however, also aware that he desperately needed some deeper direction, and so the spiritual quest became the driving motivation of his life.

For several years he became a "seeker" among the Manichees, a dualistic sect popular at the time. (The Manichees divided the world between good and evil and held that matter was inherently evil and the mind was inherently good.) He studied Neoplatonic philosophy. Finally, after dismissing it out of hand for some time, he experienced a conversion to the Christian faith, a faith broad and rich enough to engage his intellectual and creative energies, yet one that also provided focus to those energies. Augustine discovered that at the root of his restlessness was a longing for God.

✢ ✢ ✢

In the next session, we will consider some of the cultural challenges to becoming intentional about our spirituality. Following Augustine's lead, we will see later (especially in Sessions 3 and 4) how a specifically Christian spirituality can help us direct our desire to give life to others and to ourselves in healthy ways.

## Sharing Our Faith

✚ This session invites us to think about defining spirituality as the way in which we channel our energy and fire. What strikes me in this definition? For what am I longing?

✚ Rolheiser describes a healthy spirituality as one that balances order and creative chaos. Which is needed in my life right now—a little more structure or a little more zest?

✚ Share stories together of people you know personally who seem to have directed their vital energies in life-giving ways. What is it about their spirituality that I admire? How can I better direct my vital energies in life-giving ways?

## Living the Good News

*Choose how you feel the Word of God and your sharing challenge you to action for the week ahead. The best actions are always the ones that emerge from the specific contexts of your own lives and sharing. These suggested actions are just that, suggestions. If they capture your imagination and seem like the right action for your group or yourself, then proceed with one of them. If they do not, devise more appropriate individual and/or group actions.*

🌐 A quote about God from St. Augustine reads, "You have made us for yourself, O God, and our hearts are restless until they rest in you." Keep a daily or weekly journal and record the instances when your own restlessness is apparent. What form does this restlessness usually take? Note how you tend to deal with or direct that restlessness. At the end of the week, bring this prayer to God asking for guidance about how you might more satisfyingly find "rest" in your restlessness.

If you are a person who lacks discipline, commit yourself to a time each day in which you "give God space."

Consider lighting a candle each morning and saying a brief prayer for the day ahead; spend fifteen minutes reading Scripture and ponder its message; commit to going to bed (or getting up) at a reasonable hour so you will be more productive; or commit to doing a daily kind deed for someone. You may also want to "give God space" by enjoying ten minutes of daily delight: Lie on your back while enjoying beautiful music; walk in a garden or buy a bouquet and breathe in the scent of the flowers; play a game; sing a song; skip; dance.

Ask a few people outside the group, "What is spirituality?" Listen to and reflect upon their answers. Share with them your insights from this session.

Given where I am in my own life and as a response to the Word of God and our sharing, I feel called to

## Closing Prayer

*Share together prayers of intercession or praise.*
*Then pray together the following prayer:*

> God of love, Father of mercy,
> help us to be attentive
> to the deepest love currents in our lives.
> Guide our restless hearts
> and help us use our life energies
> for the glory of your name.
> Amen.

## Looking Ahead

*Prepare for your next session by prayerfully reading and studying Session 2.*

## Informal Gathering

## Suggestions for Further Reading

Robert J. Wicks, *Living a Gentle, Passionate Life*, Paulist Press

St. Augustine, *The Confessions*

Mike Aquilina, *The Way of the Fathers: Praying with the Early Christians*, Our Sunday Visitor

Mary E. Penrose, *Refreshing Water from Ancient Wells: The Wisdom of Women Mystics*, Paulist Press

Benedict J. Groeschel, C.F.R, and Kevin Perrotta., *The Journey Toward God: In the Footsteps of the Great Spiritual Writers—Catholic, Protestant and Orthodox*, Servant Publications

The United States Conference of Catholic Bishops approved in 2004 and published in 2006 the *United States Catholic Catechism for Adults*, which received the recognition of the Holy See. This *Catechism* is an adaptation of the English translation of the *Catechism of the Catholic Church*, first published in 1994, with modifications included in the 1997 edition.

The *Catechism of the Catholic Church*, which contains a rich summary of the principal elements of the faith, was meant to encourage and assist in the writing of new local catechisms. The *United States Catholic Catechism for Adults* takes into account our U.S. situation, culture, saints, and holy leaders, while carefully preserving the unity of faith and fidelity to Catholic doctrine. Where applicable, references are included for both. You can then use what the *Catechisms* offer in your sharing.

*Catechism of the Catholic Church:*
    Paragraphs 1, 355-368, 1700-1709, 1720-1724, 2683-2684

# SESSION 2

# The Challenge of Our Culture

## Sharing

*Briefly share on one of the following questions:*

"How am I right now?" or
"What good news would I like to share?"

## Sharing the Good News

*Share how you did with your action response from the last session (Living the Good News) or how you were able to incorporate the message of the last session into your daily lives.*

## Lifting Our Hearts ...

### ... in Song

*Play or sing one of the following or another song of your choice:*

"Everyday God"
"Hosea"

### ... in the Quiet

*Pause for a few moments of silence and enter more deeply into the presence of God.*

21

### ... in the Word

*Read aloud* Colossians 1:9-14.

*Take a few minutes to ponder a word, a phrase, a question, or a feeling that rises up in you. Reflect on this quietly; then share it aloud.*

*(Even if no one wishes to reflect aloud, permit sufficient time for silent reflection.)*

### ... in Prayer

*Conclude with this prayer spoken together:*

> Everyday God and Father,
> you have called creation good and
> placed us here to enjoy its beauty,
> yet we are surrounded by much
> that masquerades as beautiful
> and obscures you from our view.
> We are distracted by superficial and shallow desires,
> lured into being less than you created us to be.
> Help us remember who we truly are:
> your beloved daughters and sons.
> We ask this in Jesus' name and
> through the power of the Holy Spirit.
> Amen.

## Our Companion on the Journey

# St. Francis de Sales

> "Let us all belong to God ... in the midst of so
> much busyness brought on
> by the diversity of worldly things...."

St. Francis de Sales (17th century, France and Savoy)

IN AN ERA WHEN many people thought that only
monks and nuns could have truly spiritual lives,
Francis de Sales wrote a book, *The Introduction
to the Devout Life*, for women and men who had
ordinary workaday lives. He knew the problems
that the culture of his own day presented to the
people he guided: busyness, vanity, luxury, harmful associations forged for gain. Everyone is called
to holiness, he taught, a holiness adapted to his or
her particular life circumstances. He encouraged
housewives, grocers, and courtiers to pray, not like
monks, but in ways that flowed out of their work
and family responsibilities. He also helped them
see the ways their culture kept them from being
attentive to God's presence. De Sales was himself a
busy bishop, preacher, writer, and spiritual direc-
tor, sought after by both famous and ordinary
people. Yet he managed to keep God at the center
of all his activities.

## Encountering Wisdom for Life

WE STARTED OUR SESSION with the question, "How am
I feeling right now?" because God meets us exactly where we are, not in some idealized situation.
Our culture is part of where and how we are. We have much
to be grateful for, much to celebrate. However, many things in
our culture can militate against us channeling our desires in
life-giving ways. Many of us find it very hard to distinguish
between the random, fleeting desires that preoccupy us and
wholesome longings. We have our heads turned by all that
glitters. We find it difficult to recognize God's presence in our
lives and to respond to that presence, which is actually the
source and end of our truest desires. We get caught up in surface

longings, and our focus becomes scattered and fragmented. What might be some of the cultural reasons for this?

**Naïveté.** First, in our culture, we tend to be fairly naïve about the fiery energy we possess. Like Janis Joplin, we play pretty loose and easy with desire. We tend to resist any external force, religious or secular, that would restrict our absolute freedom to let energy flow through us. We want to accumulate things as much as possible, experience as much as possible, view whatever we want, take and use whatever we want.

Wherever we turn there are advertisements that seduce us, telling us that we have to be beautiful, admired, happy, and fulfilled. TV, magazines, video games, and films glamorize casual sex and violence of all kinds. Pornography is readily available and may entice us, convincing us that other persons exist solely for our gratification. We are pressured to taste it all and drink it all in.

Free from any guidelines, we tend to swing between being over-stimulated and being depressed. We long to be able to balance good disciplines with our limited energy. Spirituality is about finding the ways, the disciplines, by which to access that powerful energy and to contain it creatively. Spirituality is about recognizing that our deep energies come to us from God and are given to us for the flourishing of God's good world, not about shutting ourselves down. We must not be naïve about the power of our energies.

**Narcissism.** Second, in our culture, we tend to be overly self-preoccupied. Narcissism is the name we give to this cultural problem. The word comes from the ancient Greek myth that tells of Narcissus, a handsome boy who fell in love with his own reflection in a pond and, unable to tear himself away from it, he eventually pined away and died.

Our culture tends to encourage narcissism. We do like to

look out for Number One: we do want to be the center of attention; we are obsessed with winning and with self-gratification. Popular magazines extol celebrities, inviting us to emulate their lavish lifestyles. We are led to feel we must have a new or improved house, a new tractor or truck, the dream vacation, and the idealized spouse as essential components of our happiness. Some of us long for notoriety, for our exploits and our antics to be public; some of us even film our daily habits and post them on the Internet for the world to see. We spend billions of dollars annually on cosmetics, the newest fashions, and plastic surgery to produce the perfect appearance.

In contrast, a true and healthy self-love is open to others, gives as well as receives, and seeks the common good. There is, of course, a very real need to love ourselves. No one can love others if one does not know one is lovable. But love for self must be rooted in a deep reverence for life itself, not based on unattainable ideals of perfection, or a fragile, inflated self-centeredness. We love ourselves best when we become persons who can love others, as we would like to be loved.

**Pragmatism.** Third, we are a culture of pragmatists. We are enamored of practical results, with efficiency, the bottom line. While our pragmatism may serve us well in some areas, such as technological invention, it makes us forget that the value of a person is not discovered in his or her capacity to produce, but in the simple fact of being.

If we think something doesn't make money or advance our career, we often don't value it. Our pragmatism causes us to be overly focused on work, achievement, and the practical things of life, often to the exclusion of relationships with God, ourselves, our families, and our friends. We may feel as though we have to have the latest car, the biggest house, and give all our energies to acquiring these. Or, we may be caught in a situation where we must work for low wages and so find ourselves working 24/7 just to make ends meet. Either way, we find ourselves ensnared in a culture of pragmatism where an enslaving work ethic often reigns supreme.

**Restlessness.** Fourth, restlessness is a real issue. Not the God-given prompting to seek more deeply, love more truly, or live more graciously, but the restlessness that is edged with anger and contempt and born of our frantic search for more and more superficial stimulation and sensation. We may have a hard time being content with simple joys as our culture encourages us to feel dissatisfied.

We habitually fill up empty time so that we complain there is "never enough of it." We move constantly. We change addresses, jobs, friends, TV channels, and loyalties frequently. We eat and drink to excess and are greedy for new and risky experiences. We go for fast cars and extreme sports and more and more dangerous thrills. To have less and be less seems a betrayal of what our culture promises. We keep ourselves so busy and distracted that there is no room for the cultivation of a spiritual life.

Each culture offers its own challenges to the spiritual life—ours is not the only one. Four hundred years ago, Francis de Sales found himself cautioning those who consulted him to avoid the tempting but often questionable diversions of a pleasure-seeking society, the dangerous liaisons of false friendships, and the busyness that is part of engaging in business and having a family. So, we are not the only ones. But each situation is unique. The way *we* tend to be in the culture where *we* find ourselves doesn't always make it easy to be spiritual or to channel our fiery, energetic desire in life-giving ways.

✠ ✠ ✠

In our next session, we will begin to explore some of the ways we can focus our desire, ways that you may be surprised to find are already very close to your heart. But first, let us find ourselves exactly where we are. The point is not to feel guilty or discouraged about ourselves, but to come to a clear assessment of where we are. God's grace will find us there.

## Sharing Our Faith

✠ Do I find it difficult to sense God's presence in my life? What cultural factors might contribute to this? For example, have I tended to be overly focused on myself in some area of my life (narcissism), or too concerned about achievements or results (pragmatism), or overly busy, driven, impatient, and risk or thrill seeking (restlessness)?

✠ If I imagine myself at the end of my life, how do I want others to remember me?

✠ What kind of person do I genuinely long to become? What is one step I can take toward this goal?

## Living the Good News

*Choose how you feel the Word of God and your sharing challenge you to action for the week ahead. The best actions are always the ones that emerge from the specific contexts of your own lives and sharing. These suggested actions are just that, suggestions. If they capture your imagination and seem like the right action for your group or yourself, then proceed with one of them. If they do not, devise more appropriate individual and/or group actions.*

🌐 For a day, do not watch television or use a computer. (Do not impose this decision on family members who are not participants.) Notice what sort of time opens up and how you feel without the input of television or the Internet. If several members of the group do this, compare notes on the experience.

Set aside time this week to enjoy your children, spouse, grandchildren, or friends. Prepare a meal together, play board games one evening, take a picnic to the park, or participate in an outdoor activity. Do this especially if you are a person who feels compelled to be busy at every moment.

From now on when an advertisement entices you to purchase something, question the reasons why you would buy it. Make a deliberate effort to question and seek out genuine reasons before being blindly persuaded by advertising.

Reach out to another through a call, visit, or mail, as you would like someone to reach out to you.

Cultivate your spiritual life by scheduling and spending quiet time with God each day or at least a few times this week.

Make a list of all the purchases you have made in the last month or week. Next to each purchase indicate whether it was something you or your family genuinely needed or whether it was something you merely wanted. Bring the question of need or want to the purchases you make next week.

Given where I am in my own life and as a response to the Word of God and our sharing, I feel called to

_____

_____

✠ ✠ ✠

## Closing Prayer

*Share together prayers of intercession, petition, or praise.*
*Then pray together the Lord's Prayer, followed by this prayer*
*spoken together:*

> Loving Father, we seek the simplicity of your love
> in the midst of our complex culture.
> Teach us to be able to know the difference
> between what we need and what we want.
> May your wisdom guide us in our search
> and in our actions.
> We pray through Jesus Christ and
> in the power of the Holy Spirit.
> Amen.

## Looking Ahead

*Prepare at home for your next session by prayerfully reading and*
*studying Session 3.*

## Informal Gathering

## SUGGESTIONS FOR FURTHER READING

Tom Beaudoin, *Consuming Faith:*
*Integrating Who We Are with What We Buy,*
Sheed & Ward

St. Francis de Sales, *Introduction to the Devout Life*

Joseph F. Power, O.S.F.S., *Francis de Sales:*
*Finding God Wherever You Are: Selected Spiritual Writings,*
New City Press

*United States Catholic Catechism for Adults:*
Chapter 2. God Comes to Meet Us

*Catechism of the Catholic Church:*
Paragraphs 293-294, 1718-1724, 1763-1770

# Spirituality in a Christian Context

## Love of God and Neighbor

## Sharing

*Briefly share on one of the following questions:*

"How am I right now?" or
"What good news would I like to share?"

## Sharing the Good News

*Share how you did with your action response from the last session (Living the Good News) or how you were able to incorporate the message of the last session into your daily lives.*

## Lifting Our Hearts ...

### ... in Song

*Play or sing one of the following or another song of your choice:*
"Anthem"
"I Have Loved You"

### ... in the Quiet

*Pause for a few moments of silence and enter more deeply into the presence of God.*

## ... in the Word

*Read aloud* Psalm 100.

*Take a few minutes to ponder a word, a phrase, a question, or a feeling that rises up in you. Reflect on this quietly; then share it aloud.*

*(Even if no one wishes to reflect aloud, permit sufficient time for silent reflection.)*

## ... in Prayer

*Conclude with this prayer spoken together:*

> Gracious God,
> you are a circle of love.
> In you we discover our beginning
> and the end of our longing.
> Help us always to be mindful
> that we are yours.
> Amen.

## Our Companion on the Journey

# Julian of Norwich

> "For we are so preciously loved by God
> that we cannot even comprehend it.
> No created being can ever know
> how much and how sweetly and tenderly
> God loves them."

Julian of Norwich (14th century, England)

WE HAVE VERY LITTLE biographical information about Dame Julian of Norwich,
except that she lived in a cell attached to a church
in Norwich, England. Julian lived in the 1300s,
one of the most tumultuous of centuries: plague,
famine, and violent warfare sent countless num-
bers of people to early graves. Although she spent
most of her time in prayer, during part of the
day, Julian would come to her window and speak
with the people who came for spiritual counsel.
We do know that in her prayer she experienced a
series of "showings" or visions from God, which
she continued to reflect on for years. At the core
of these showings was the intimate knowledge
of God's closeness or "kinship" with us and the
tenderness with which we are loved. God, Julian
tells us, is a circle of love, the Trinity, who is our
maker, our keeper, and our lover. She shared her
deeply compelling Christian vision with all who
came seeking her counsel.

## Encountering Wisdom for Life

WE'VE HAD SOME TIME NOW to reflect on the fact that as
human beings we each have an energy, a life force
most often experienced as longing, that needs to
be channeled in life-giving ways. Additionally, we have named
for ourselves some of the challenges that our particular culture
poses to working on that task, challenges that keep us focused
on superficial desires and mask the deeper longings at the root
of our lives.

The next step is to explore the *how* of this task. All the great
religious traditions of the world have attempted to guide their

adherents toward life-giving beliefs and practices. Clearly this is a deep-felt need, as evidenced by bookstore shelves lined with titles claiming to explain this *how*.

What about us as Christians? As followers of Jesus, we need to look closely at the ways that Jesus Christ and the community that claims discipleship in his name have framed the task of directing the deep longing that insistently tugs at each of us. This involves much more than asking, "What would Jesus do?" It involves an understanding of the deepest meaning of the Christian story. The story is first and foremost, a love story.

It might be summarized in the following way. Our loving God created this beautiful world. Although we human beings were created in the divine image, we do not always realize this—we fail to love as we have been loved, we sin. Yet out of love God has approached us, God became one with us in a unique way in the person of Jesus in order to bring us back into loving relationship with him and with each other. Jesus the Christ showed us the way we are loved and how we must love one another.

That divine love was and is so powerful that it is victorious over every other power in the world, including death. This powerful love continues to live on through the power of the Spirit who animates the community of the faithful, the Church, which is the Body of Christ in the world. The Spirit works in us as community and as individuals as we are guided, comforted, and inspired to realize our truest selves and to live with one another in love. For Christians, one way to describe the spiritual life is being responsive to the inspiration and challenges of the Holy Spirit.

In *The Holy Longing*, Fr. Rolheiser explores the spiritual implications of the Christian story. Having been loved with infinite tenderness, having discovered that God is both the source and end point of our deepest longing, we make a response. Our spirituality is, we recall, what we do with the fire burning within.

It is about how we love in return. Rolheiser suggests that there are several components necessary for any spirituality that takes the love story of the triune God and humanity seriously. These components are rooted firmly in the biblical witness. The essentials for a healthy spiritual life as he outlines them are four: personal prayer and morality, social justice, mellowness of heart, and community. In this session, we will look at the first two of these components: personal prayer and morality and then social justice. In Session 4, we will explore the third and fourth: mellowness of heart and community.

**Personal Prayer and Morality.** Jesus asks us to "pray ... in secret," (Matthew 6:6) to have a personal relationship with him, and through him, with God. If you read the Scriptures you find that this intimate relationship is not simply a question of feeling warm about Jesus but of keeping the commandments. "If you love me, you will keep my commandments" (John 14:15). Christianity is not merely about specific external behaviors or abstract ideas; it is about a dynamic engagement with the living God. Such an engagement asks that we take our faith to heart, that we make it deeply our own, so that it becomes a part of the fabric of our daily life.

Personal prayer, in its many forms, is how we engage in an intimate way with God. Prayer is the language of our love relationship with God. Julian of Norwich, seven centuries ago, grasped this truth firmly. In one of her "showings" she records, "God showed me a sight of his familiar love ... He showed me something small, no bigger than a hazelnut, lying in the palm of my hand ... I thought, what can this be? ... And I was given this general answer: It is everything which is made ... In this little thing I saw three properties. The first is that God made it, the second is that God loves it, the third is that God preserves it." In personal prayer, God often gives us deep insights in a simple way.

Additionally, just as we cannot give our love fully to our loved ones if our lives are disordered, so neither can we give ourselves fully to God and others. Morality involves taking seriously the call to personal integrity. The Ten Commandments and the Beatitudes are the basic guidelines ordering the Christian life, as is the "new command" Jesus gave to his friends at the Last Supper: "[L]ove one another. Just as I have loved you, you also should love one another" (John 13:34).

**Social Justice.** Jesus' teaching on our obligation to create justice so that the poor must be raised up is as much an essential component of his teaching as is personal prayer and morality. He picks up the theme of the Jewish prophets who taught that the quality of people's faith can be measured by how the most vulnerable—widows, orphans, strangers—are treated. So where we stand with God depends not just on our prayer and good faith, but also on where we stand with those who are poor and marginalized.

Scripture challenges us to make a special option for those who suffer, not simply by giving of our excess but by helping to create a world that is more just. In the Gospel of Matthew, Jesus tells his disciples that at the last judgment those who will share in the kingdom prepared by the Son of Man will merit because "I was hungry and you gave me food, I was thirsty and you gave me something to drink, I was a stranger and you welcomed me, I was naked and you gave me clothing, I was sick and you took care of me, I was in prison and you visited me." (Matthew 25:35-36). The disciples were as amazed by this obligation as we might be and wondered, "When did we see you?" Jesus' answer is simple, "[J]ust as you did it to one of the least of these who are members of my family, you did it to me" (Matthew 25:40).

What is crucial here is to become aware that when we care for those who are poor and marginalized, we are not simply doing a good deed for some stranger who falls outside our normal purview.

What Jesus and the prophets call us to is the recognition that we are all part of a whole. We have responsibility not only for our immediate family and friends, but also for God's world. We are called not only to give aid to those in need but to help create conditions in which the poverty, misery, and violence that deface so much of God's creatures and creation no longer exist.

Jesus offers us a summation of all the wisdom found in the law and the prophets in what have become known as the two great commands (Matthew 22:34-40): to love God with all one's heart and mind and to love one's neighbor as oneself. Our intimate life with God and our life with each other are undeniably linked. The striking thing is that, far from being "commands" that are troublesome, the two great commands are the answer to the longing that lies deep in our hearts.

Love of God and love of one another these are the commands that outline the sure path that can help us direct the energy that burns inside us. The great tenderness of Julian's vision of a world and everything in it created and sustained in love is one we are called to embrace. We are, so to speak, to see what God sees and to love as God loves.

## Sharing Our Faith

✠ How can my prayer for others be more closely linked by my actions on behalf of them?

✠ Consider the gifts you have received from God. Think perhaps of the beautiful earth, family, talents, meaningful work, friends, faith, or life itself. In what ways have I responded to God's love or how have I reached out to others with my gifts?

✠ Who are the most vulnerable in our society today? In what ways can I or we reach out to help?

## Living the Good News

*Choose how you feel the Word of God and your sharing challenge you to action for the week ahead. The best actions are always the ones that emerge from the specific contexts of your own lives and sharing. These suggested actions are just that, suggestions. If they capture your imagination and seem like the right action for your group or yourself, then proceed with one of them. If they do not, devise more appropriate individual and/or group actions.*

If you do not already find time for personal prayer, set aside five minutes each day to pray, preferably at a not-too-busy time. You may like to use one of the prayers from this week's session, read the scripture passage over again, listen to the song that accompanies the session, or simply sit quietly and share with God what is in your heart.

Take the time to appreciate God's good earth. Perhaps you might take a drive in the country as a group or alone. Go apple picking; take a hike or a bike ride; walk by a lake, a river, or at the seashore; enjoy the flowers at a local park if weather permits. Enjoy the experience; be glad the gift of life is yours. Perhaps write a prayer about it or take a prayer photo.

Choose a current issue of importance. Become familiar with legislation that will work creatively for just structures or solutions. Contact your representatives and urge them to pass such legislation.

Spend some time in prayer and reading Scripture, asking God to reveal to you who are the most vulnerable in your circle of family, friends, neighbors, or co-workers. Reach out to those who most strongly or persistently come to mind.

Be a voice for those in our society who are not heard or whose voice has no sway among those influenced by the established citizenry. Write a letter or call your legislators this week. You might want to make this a regular practice.

As a group, talk about who in your neighborhood, city, or town is most vulnerable. Decide to reach out together.

Review the Ten Commandments and the Beatitudes. Decide which one(s) needs more attention in your life and determine with God's help to live that commandment or beatitude more generously. (See Matthew 5:1-12 and the *Catechism of the Catholic Church*, #2052.)

Given where I am in my own life and as a response to the Word of God and our sharing, I feel called to

## Closing Prayer

*Pray together the following prayer:*

> Good and gracious God,
> you create and sustain us.
> May we be mindful of the gifts you have given.
> May the fire that burns in us
> burn more fiercely
> with gratitude and the longing to respond
> to the promptings of the Spirit.
> We ask this through Jesus and the Holy Spirit.
> Amen.

## Looking Ahead

*Prepare at home for your next session by prayerfully reading and studying Session 4.*

## Informal Gathering

### SUGGESTIONS FOR FURTHER READING

Phyllis Zagano, *On Prayer: A Letter to My Godchild,*
   Liguori Publications

John C. Endres and Elizabeth Liebert, *A Retreat with the Psalms: Resources for Personal and Communal Prayer,*
   Paulist Press

Julian of Norwich, *Showings*, Paulist Press

Julian, John Kirvin and Richard Chilson, *All Will Be Well: Based on the Classic Spirituality of Julian of Norwich,* 30 Days with a Great Spiritual Teacher Series,
   Ave Maria Press

Thomas Merton, *New Seeds of Contemplation*
   New Directions Publishing Corp.

*United States Catholic Catechism for Adults:*
   Chapter 35. God Calls Us to Pray;
   Chapters 23. Life in Christ—Part One

*Catechism of the Catholic Church:*
   Paragraphs 1716-1729, 1886-1948, 2052-2082, 2093-2557, 2558-2567, 2598-2622

# Spirituality in a Christian Context

## A Heart for God and Each Other

## Sharing

*Briefly share on one of the following questions:*

"How am I right now?" or
"What good news would I like to share?"

## Sharing the Good News

*Share how you did with your action response from the last session
(Living the Good News) or how you were able to incorporate the
message of the last session into your daily lives.*

## Lifting Our Hearts ...

### ... in Song

*Play or sing one of the following or another song of your choice:*

"E Haku I Ka Pu'u Wai" ("Weave One Heart")
"Jesus, the Lord"

### ... in the Quiet

*Pause for a few moments of silence and enter more deeply into the
presence of God.*

## ... in the Word

*Read aloud* John 11:17-27.

*Take a few minutes to ponder a word, a phrase, a question, or a feeling that rises up in you. Reflect on this quietly; then share it aloud.*

*(Even if no one wishes to reflect aloud, permit sufficient time for silent reflection.)*

## ... in Prayer

*Conclude with this prayer spoken together:*

> Loving Lord Jesus,
> with Martha and Mary we claim you
> as guide, friend, and way.
> May we have ears to hear your call,
> eyes to see you where we do not expect you,
> and hearts spacious enough to welcome all.
> Amen.

## Our Companion on the Journey

# St. Patrick

> "Christ with me, Christ before me,
> Christ behind me, Christ within me,
> Christ beneath me, Christ above me,
> Christ at my right, Christ at my left ...
> Christ in the heart of every one who thinks of me,
> Christ in the mouth of every one who speaks to me,
> Christ in every eye that sees me."

St. Patrick (4th century, Ireland)

PATRICK, THE PATRON SAINT of Ireland, was born in the late fourth century in Scotland to a non-Christian family. At the age of 16, he was sold into slavery by a group of Irish marauders that raided his village. During his captivity, he experienced a conversion to God. Escaping from slavery, he went to Gaul where he received monastic training. He then returned to Ireland to undertake the work of preaching the Christian Gospel. His mission in Ireland, where he served as a bishop, lasted for thirty years. This prayer, known as the "Breastplate of St. Patrick," reflects the saint's sense of the power of Christ and his desire to immerse himself in that powerful presence.

## Encountering Wisdom for Life

THE CHRISTIAN STORY is a love story of God's overwhelming goodness. At its center is Jesus, the Christ, who shows us the way God loves and invites us to do the same. We are asked to "pray in secret" to cultivate a loving relationship with our good God in prayer and through the moral ordering of our lives. We are also asked to help bring about a just world in which all are able to share equitably. In this session we will explore two other "essential components" of a Christian spirituality: they are mellowness of heart and community as a fundamental element of true worship.

**Mellowness of Heart.** The Christian life is not all prayer and sacrifice. It is also a life aware of the gifts and joys God gives us. We must let our lives be filled with those things (good friendships, creativity, celebrating, and healthy leisure) that allow us to delight in the goodness of being alive. Only one kind of person transforms the world spiritually, Rolheiser tells us, someone with a grateful heart. Gratitude is as essential to a holy life as are believing and doing the right things. If we are consumed by anger and bitterness, if we are so full of zeal and righteous indignation that we become hardhearted, if we are wired, anxious, and workaholic, we may be too closed in on ourselves to be grateful and delight in the goodness God offers us.

When we trust enough in the God of love, we are more able to extend that love to all. The famous parable of the Prodigal Son (Luke 15:11-32) illustrates this essential truth. You will remember there are two sons, one who has taken his inheritance and squandered it in frivolous ways and another who has been dutiful and remained at his father's side. The "prodigal" son regrets his folly and seeks the father's mercy, offering to be taken back into the household as a slave. Instead, the father opens his heart and welcomes him back as a son with a great feast, much to the dismay of the dutiful son, who felt he had justly earned the father's attention.

Jesus helps us to understand that we can be estranged from the father's house in more than one way. We can stray through infidelity and weakness (like the younger son) or through bitterness and resentment (like the older son). The father, in this scriptural lesson, has the kind of empathy that comes from an unconditionally loving heart, which enables his mercy. His gratitude at having his son back overcomes any resentment of wrongdoing. Mellowness also implies that we are flexible and forgiving, willing to put aside our preconceived ideas or plans, willing to reconsider, willing to let love be the compass that directs our relationships and our lives. Such a heart is a heart that has allowed God's love to enter it and change its behavior.

**Community.** The Gospel clearly teaches that God calls us, not just as individuals, but as a community and that how we relate to each other is just as essential as how we relate to God. In

Matthew 22:34-40, Jesus is shown summarizing the whole of the law and the prophets for a group of skeptical teachers by declaring that the two great commandments, to love God and love one's neighbor, can never be separated. We can really love God who is love only if we are concretely engaged with a living faith community. We do not fruitfully worship alone.

We are taught, nurtured, challenged, and supported in the spiritual life by all the levels of our faith community. The gathered worshiping Church, devout reception of the sacraments, the variety of small faith-sharing groups, individual relationships of spiritual care: all these are essential parts of our Christian journeys. They provide a wide and solid grounding for our personal search. In community we are not only supported and guided, but we are challenged and offered resources for our spiritual journey. The search for God is not a private search for what is ultimate for oneself, but rather a communal search for the face of God. Whatever the struggles of being community might be, it is the context in which our faith best grows; it is the context in which our hearts are shaped by loving God who is love.

**Patrick's Mellowness of Heart and Community.** Among the works attributed to St. Patrick is his "Declaration of the Great Works of God." In it he tells of his missionary travels dedicated to creating a Christian community in Ireland, and he praises God for his strength, majesty, and righteousness. Patrick does so because he understands that a disciple and a recipient of God's grace is given a song to sing, a testimony to proclaim, and a full heart that overflows with gratitude. Patrick understood the effect of gratitude on our spiritual growth. He knew his own joy was something he could share and that our love for God was best revealed when our prayer and praise rise up in chorus and resound together.

In keeping with Rolheiser's theory that someone with a grateful heart transforms the world spiritually, we need only to reflect on the life and work of Patrick to see this come into action. The gratitude that Patrick expressed as a benefit of God's presence in his life leads to mellowness of heart. It reduces the struggle we face when restlessness or dissatisfaction dominate our lives. Appreciating the gifts of God's presence in our lives can be a transforming aspect through which we become much more generous and willing to give. Having a grateful heart brings about peace and healing.

**Personal Prayer and Morality, Social Justice, Mellowness of Heart, Community.** These four not only comprise the essence of the Christian spiritual life, they supply its balance as well. These are the four essentials of an authentic Christian spirituality as Rolheiser outlines them. We are not expected to be all things to all persons. We are not all asked to pray with the zeal of monks, or to go off to faraway mission fields, or to be cheery saints, or to spend endless hours doing volunteer service for the Church. What matters is that the channeling of the deep fire within us has both a personal and a communal dimension.

God calls us to love. We love well by spending intimate time with the One who so loves us. And we love well by loving others, especially those who are neglected and in need, who are as deeply loved by God as we are. Just as in any love relationship, we need to cultivate gratitude, to have "mellowness of heart," and the ability to delight in the goodness given us. Finally, we need the support and guidance of each other. To love well is both an intimate and a shared task.

## Sharing Our Faith

✙ Tell of a time you have experienced mellowness of heart (that is, a heart that has allowed God's love to enter it). How can I find more time to experience mellowness of heart in the midst of the busyness of my life?

- To what extent does my life emphasize a value in being part of community? What expectations and demands that come from being part of community are most difficult for me to deal with?
- What, if any, are the components that are missing from my own spiritual practice? Personal prayer and morality? Social justice and action? Mellowness of heart? Community? Explain.
- What can I do about what is missing? (Try to be practical and explicit, but also be honest. During this next period of time before meeting again, ask God in prayer to give greater insight into the ways of becoming a closer follower of Jesus.)

## Living the Good News

*Choose how you feel the Word of God and your sharing challenge you to action for the week ahead. The best actions are always the ones that emerge from the specific contexts of your own lives and sharing. These suggested actions are just that, suggestions. If they capture your imagination and seem like the right action for your group or yourself, then proceed with one of them. If they do not, devise more appropriate individual and/or group actions.*

- Keep a daily journal for a week recording the times you have found yourself intensely bothered by others' actions or speech. At the end of the week, pray with your journal. Ask God to help you acquire greater "mellowness of heart." Perhaps you will need to imagine the person or people involved differently, seeing them with the eyes of the heart that knows them as God's own children too. Determine how you will follow through your reflections in your daily living.

Spend some time in a natural setting (park, garden, seashore, woodland, mountain, lake, desert, etc.) or in a place that is meaningful to you (church, museum, school, aquarium). Take your book with you and pray Francis of Assisi's *Canticle of Brother Sun* (see pages 49-50). Then find your own words to express to God your gratitude for the beauty of the earth. Attentiveness to the beauty of the world can be part of your developing "mellowness of heart."

Arrange to visit, either as a group or alone, a local family homeless shelter or nursing care facility. Ask the staff to help you understand the reasons people find themselves at these institutions and how you can contribute to their well-being.

If you do not already do this, attend a program or event that puts you in contact with your community beyond the group you usually associate with. This may be a parish event or a neighborhood gathering.

Cultivate gratitude by spending time in prayer thanking God for every gift you have received and by expressing your thanks as others reach out to you.

Reflect on the suggested action in the last question in **Sharing Our Faith**. Journal the ways you might become a closer follower of Jesus. Then weekly, go back to your list and see how you are doing.

Given where I am in my own life and as a response to the Word of God and our sharing, I feel called to

# St. Francis of Assisi's
## *Canticle of Brother Sun*

Most High, all powerful and good Lord,
to you are due the praises, the glory,
the honor and every blessing.
To you only, O highest one, are they due
and no human being is worthy to speak of you.

Be praised, my Lord, with all your creatures
especially by brother sun
by whom we are lightened every day,
for he is fair and radiant with great splendor
and bears your likeness, O highest one.

Be praised, my Lord, for sister moon and the stars.
You have set them in heaven, precious, fair and bright.

Be praised, my Lord, by brother wind
and by air and cloud and sky and every weather
through whom you give life to all your creatures.

Be praised, my Lord, by sister water
for she is useful and humble and precious and chaste.

Be praised, my Lord, by brother fire.
By him we are lightened at night
and he is fair and cheerful and sturdy and strong.

Be praised, my Lord, by our sister, mother earth.
She sustains and governs us
and brings forth many fruits and
   colored flowers and plants.

Be praised, my Lord,
   by those who have been pardoned by your love
and who bear infirmity and tribulation.
Blessed are those who suffer them in peace
for by you, O highest one, they shall be crowned.

Be praised, my Lord, by our sister, physical death
from whom no one who lives can escape...
Blessed are those who are found
   in your most holy will
for the second death can do them no harm.

May I bless and praise you, my Lord,
   and give you thanks
and serve you with great humility.

## Closing Prayer

*Share together prayers of intercession, thanksgiving, or praise.*

*Then pray together:*

> Father, you are tender with our shortcomings.
> Take us gently by the hand
> and do not ever let us go.
> Keep leading and we will follow.
> We make this prayer in the name of Jesus
> and in the power of the Holy Spirit.
> Amen.

## Looking Ahead

*Prepare at home for your next session by prayerfully reading and studying Session 5.*

## Informal Gathering

## Suggestions for Further Reading

Robert Ellsberg, *The Saints' Guide to Happiness,*
  Farrar, Straus and Giroux

David Steindl-Rast, *Gratefulness, the Heart of Prayer:*
  *An Approach to Life in Fullness*, Paulist Press

Thomas O'Loughlin, *Journeys on the Edges: The Celtic Tradition,*
  Traditions of Christian Spirituality Series, Orbis Books

Timothy Joyce, O.S.B., *A Retreat with Patrick:*
  *Discovering God in All*, A Retreat With Series,
  St. Anthony Messenger Press

# Incarnation

## Christ in Us

## Sharing

*Briefly share on one of the following questions:*

"How am I right now?" or
"What good news would I like to share?"

## Sharing the Good News

*Share how you did with your action response from the last session (Living the Good News) or how you were able to incorporate the message of the last session into your daily lives.*

## Lifting Our Hearts ...

### ... in Song

*Play or sing one of the following or another song of your choice:*

"I Am For You"
"Lord, You Have Come" / "Pescador de Hombres"

### ... in the Quiet

*Pause for a few moments of silence and enter more deeply into the presence of God.*

### ... in the Word

*Read aloud* Colossians 1:24-29.

*Take a few minutes to ponder a word, a phrase, a question, or a feeling that rises up in you. Reflect on this quietly; then share it aloud.*

*(Even if no one wishes to reflect aloud, permit sufficient time for silent reflection.)*

### ... in Prayer

*Conclude with this prayer spoken together:*

> God of the call,
> like the disciples who heard themselves summoned
> who left their nets on the seashore to follow Jesus,
> let us be bold enough to do the same,
> to leave behind the narrow selves
> that cannot imagine we are called
> to be the Body of Christ in our world.
> Amen.

## Our Companion on the Journey

# St. Teresa of Avila

> "Christ has no body now but yours,
> No hands, no feet on earth but yours,
> Yours are the eyes through which he looks
> compassion on this world,
> Yours are the feet
> with which he walks to do good,
> Yours are the hands
> with which he blesses all the world.
> Yours are the hands, yours are the feet,

Yours are the eyes, you are his body.
Christ has no body now but yours,
No hands, no feet on earth but yours,
Yours are the eyes, with which he looks
compassion on the world.
Christ has no body now on earth but yours."

Teresa of Avila (16th century, Spain)

TERESA OF AVILA is remembered in many ways: as a reformer of the Carmelite monastic order, as a gifted spiritual writer, as one of three women declared Doctor by the Church because of the fullness of her teaching. But a more intimate image of this sixteenth century woman that has come down to us is of Teresa, in advanced age, in the midst of one of her innumerable long and arduous road trips undertaken on behalf of her reformed community, her carriage mired in mud during a pelting rainstorm. "If this is the way you treat your friends," she is quoted as saying to the Lord, "no wonder you have so few!" The image reveals both Teresa's earthy sense of humor and her indomitable spirit. Neither age, nor inclement weather, nor the seemingly insurmountable obstacles that she faced in her work, could deter her from the work to which she felt called—to be Christ's body in the world.

## Encountering Wisdom for Life

THE GREAT "MYSTERIES" of the Christian faith—the Trinity, the Incarnation, the Paschal Mystery (death and resurrection), Pentecost—are not merely abstract ideas or historical occurrences. They are deep truths into which we are invited. They are truths that, as a consequence of our baptism, we are charged to live out. At Christmas time we proclaim, "Emmanuel ... 'God is with us'" (Matthew 1:23). Christmas is, of course, the feast of the birth of Jesus. More importantly, it is the celebration of the Incarnation, the "enfleshment," God-with-us. A gift is given to us, but the gift is not like an expensive ornamental vase to be put on a shelf for admiration. Nor is it only like a receipt given to us of a gift received long ago, something we already enjoy. The gift of the Incarnation is more aptly seen as a wonderful suit of clothes to be worn or, more aptly still, the gift of a powerful potential that we are asked to give flesh—our flesh—to.

**We Are the Body of Christ.** In us and through us God physically continues to walk the face of the earth—just as Jesus did. At the Ascension, Jesus left the earth, but the Body of Christ remains. *We* are the Body of Christ today. *We* are God's incarnational presence.

Teresa of Avila, way back in the sixteenth century, knew this well. For many years after she entered the Carmelite convent, she lived faithfully according to the community rule. Yet she found it was not enough for her to simply go through the motions, even the motions required of a nun! She was not content to simply *say* prayers; she wanted her life to *be* a prayer, just as Jesus' life had been a prayer to God the Father.

Teresa hungered to live so intensely with and for God that she would become the arms and hands and feet God needed to renew the Church of her day. She began with her own order. The convent to which she belonged was not a scandalous one, though it was closely tied to the interests of the wealthy families who supported it. The nuns brought with them into the community the honor and titles that had distinguished them in the world.

In Teresa's mind, the Carmelite community should not exist for the sake of its wealthy patrons and their enhancement, but for God. She put into action her reforming ideas, which she believed (and others supported this belief) were prompted by God. Traveling ceaselessly over the length and breadth of Spain, Teresa was quite literally Christ's arms and legs—the Incarnation in her own part of the world. Her reform aimed to heal the wounds of religious life and the Spanish Christian society of her day. By virtue of our baptism, we, too, are called to be Christ's arms and legs—the Incarnation—wherever we can be in the world.

**The Incarnation as Healing and Reconciliation.** If we look to the witness of Scripture, we see that living out the Incarnation has certain characteristics. Throughout the Gospels, we see Jesus using his hands to heal. Over and over we see him using his touch to heal those who are blind and afflicted. These are not simply stories about Jesus' special power, although they are that, too. They are also stories about the power or energy of the Incarnation, God's healing presence at work in the world. Thus they are exemplary stories for us. To be Christ's Body we must be healers. We heal when we bind up wounds of all sorts— emotional, relational, spiritual, as well as physical.

In addition to being a healing one, Jesus' touch is reconciling. He reconciles sinners and outcasts, bringing them into community. The Gospel of Luke especially shows us Jesus inviting all sorts of alienated people to learn of the transforming power of the merciful God. He invites into his reconciling community people of questionable reputation, sinners of all sorts, and outsiders who were despised and shunned (Luke 5:27-32; 7:36-50; 19:10). As Jesus' presence was a healing and reconciling one, so must ours be.

But, you say, who am I to heal, to reconcile? Of course, we don't do this on our own power. We come to be healers by first being healed; reconcilers by first being reconciled.

One of the most telling stories is found in the Gospel of Mark. A woman, who has suffered from internal bleeding for years and has not found healing, dares to reach out from the midst of a crowd and touch the hem of Jesus' garment. Because of the cultural taboo against contact with blood, her ailment had kept her isolated from the community for all that time. If she just touches him, she hopes, she will be healed. She does, and she is. Sensing the power leave him, Jesus turns and asks who touched him. When the woman comes forward and explains, Jesus confirms her hope and says, "Daughter, your faith has made you well" (Mark 5:34). She is both healed and able now to be reconciled with her community.

The story of this hemorrhaging woman is one from which we can learn. Our healing, too, happens when we reach out to touch the Body of Christ. Through relationship with the sacraments and the liturgy of the faith community, we touch a deep source of God's healing power. We allow ourselves to be fed by the Word and by Christ's body and blood, to be cleansed by the healing action of God's forgiveness, to be open to hope and the fullness of life promised to us.

In turn, we are asked to extend this same powerful healing to others. It is not our own limited power we call on to do this, but the power of divine love that flows through us. We are asked to give flesh to—to incarnate—God's healing presence. We are asked to seek reconciliation with those from whom we are estranged. We are even asked to struggle to love and reconcile with those who are our enemies. We are not asked to condone the sinful or harmful actions enemies may have committed, but to come to honor their deepest identity as creatures whose source and final end are meant to be God.

**Incarnation: Being with and for Each Other.** In our seeking to extend healing and be reconciled, we return again and again to the source of our own healing. The community of faith, past and present, the Body of Christ, becomes a source of guidance. From Scripture, tradition, the saints, teachers, preachers, spiritual directors, wise friends, faith-sharing groups, those in

the pews around us, we learn. We seek counsel and encourage-
ment, challenge and support. What this means is that the Body
of Christ is not simply a source of our individual healing. The
Incarnation is a glimpse into the mystery of the God who is
three in one, the Trinity. While Christianity affirms that God
in essence is one, still that oneness is dynamic, a communion
of interpenetrating love. Similarly, we are never fully ourselves
just by ourselves. It is only when we are in dynamic, life-giving
relationships that we are most fully what we were created to be:
the image and likeness of God.

Community is essential to Christianity and thus to a Christian spirituality. We are called to discipleship not merely alone
but as a group. Jesus himself always called others to him and
commanded them to love one another as he had loved them
(John 15:12). Most of us are aware, as were the first disciples,
that community is never easy. The Church as we experience it is
not the glorified Body of Christ in heaven but the flawed body
of believers here on earth. Yet the Incarnation challenges us to
the truth that it is not possible to love the unseen God, if we do
not engage in the struggle to love a neighbor who can be seen:
family members, co-workers, the people who live next door, the
strangers who live on the other side of town, the "others" all
across the globe created by the good and gracious God. A Christian spirituality is always as much about dealing with each other
as dealing with God.

To follow Jesus, to be the Body of Christ in the world, is not
primarily about keeping a tally of other people's sins, passing
out religious tracts, establishing television stations to get the
good news out, or even trying to baptize everyone into the faith.
Discipleship is first and foremost about radiating and manifest-
ing the love of God as shown to us in Jesus. As disciples, we are
to form our flesh, to be transformed from the inside by God's
healing and reconciliation, so that we can give a human face to
divine love in our actions with others.

## Sharing Our Faith

✠ Tell of an instance when someone was "Christ" for you.

✠ How consciously do I reflect the fact that "Christ has no body now but mine" today? How does this realization influence my relationships and actions?

✠ How might I be an agent of God's healing and reconciling power in my personal, everyday world? If appropriate, consider how you might bring healing to the personal, local, and global levels.

✠ As part of the Body of Christ alive in the world today, how can I become a better instrument of healing and reconciliation? Be explicit.

## Living the Good News

*Choose how you feel the Word of God and your sharing challenge you to action for the week ahead. The best actions are always the ones that emerge from the specific contexts of your own lives and sharing. These suggested actions are just that, suggestions. If they capture your imagination and seem like the right action for your group or yourself, then proceed with one of them. If they do not, devise more appropriate individual and/or group actions.*

🌐 Consider an action that would heal a broken relationship. First, ask God to help you understand your part in the rupture. Perhaps, if the situation calls for this, you can write a letter, make a phone call or a personal visit initiating a process that would lead to healing.

🌐 Determine a specific way in which you will be Christ for another this week.

If you are in need of healing and have not done so already, join a support group for the grieving, divorced, widowed, and for other needs.

Contact the Project Rachel office in your diocese, or its equivalent, and ask how you can "spread the word" about the Church's post-abortion reconciliation and healing outreach. Or make contact with the National Office.

**The National Office of Post-Abortion Reconciliation and Healing, Inc.**

PO Box 07477
Milwaukee, WI 53207-0477

*National Referral line:* 800-5WE-CARE
*Business line:* 414-483-4141
*Websites:* www.noparh.com
www.menandabortion.info
*Email:* noparh@yahoo.com

As a group, find out what kinds of civic or parish opportunities are available in your local community for the work of reconciliation. Perhaps these might focus on problems of racial and ethnic discrimination or community violence. Become involved.

Spend some quiet time in prayerful adoration in the presence of the Blessed Sacrament asking Jesus to open your heart to be a healing and reconciling presence for others.

Given where I am in my own life and as a response to the Word of God and our sharing, I feel called to

## Closing Prayer

*Share together prayers of intercession, petition, or praise.*

*Then pray together the Lord's Prayer, followed by this prayer spoken together:*

>Jesus, LORD who heals,
>who binds up wounds,
>who brings us together,
>who loves us into the fullness of life,
>may we come to know ourselves
>as your own body,
>your hands,
>your eyes,
>your heart,
>to bind the wounds of the world.
>We make our prayer in Jesus' name and
>through the power of the Holy Spirit.
>Amen.

## Looking Ahead

*Prepare at home for your next session by prayerfully reading and studying Session 6.*

## Informal Gathering

## SUGGESTIONS FOR FURTHER READING

Jean Vanier, *Becoming Human,*
    Paulist Press

Michael Downey, *Hope Begins Where Hope Begins,*
    Orbis Books

St. Teresa of Avila, *The Interior Castle* or
    *The Life of St. Teresa of Avila*

Rosemary Broughton, *Praying with Teresa of Avila,*
    Companions for the Journey Series,
    St. Mary's Press

*United States Catholic Catechism for Adults:*
    Chapter 8. The Good News: God Has Sent His Son

*Catechism of the Catholic Church:*
    Paragraphs 787-796, 1114-1121, 1878-1917,
    1939-1942, 2044-2046

# The Paschal Mystery

## The Offer of New Life

## Sharing

*Briefly share on one of the following questions:*

"How am I right now?" or
"What good news would I like to share?"

## Sharing the Good News

*Share how you did with your action response from the last session (Living the Good News) or how you were able to incorporate the message of the last session into your daily lives.*

## Lifting Our Hearts ...

### ... in Song

*Play or sing one of the following or another song of your choice:*

"Join in the Dance"
"Eye Has Not Seen"

### ... in the Quiet

*Pause for a few moments of silence and enter more deeply into the presence of God.*

## ... in the Word

*Read aloud* John 12:24.

*Take a few minutes to ponder a word, a phrase, a question, or a feeling that rises up in you. Reflect on this quietly; then share it aloud.*

*(Even if no one wishes to reflect aloud, permit sufficient time for silent reflection.)*

## ... in Prayer

*Conclude with this prayer spoken together:*

> Lord Jesus,
> we hold your dying and your rising close to our hearts.
> May we sense that we are part of this mystery.
> May we have the courage and the grace
> to trust that, even in hardship,
> your transforming love never fails.
> Amen.

## Our Companion on the Journey

# St. Elizabeth Ann Seton

"What a comfort—the black clouds I foresee may pass by harmless
or if in that Providence of grace, they fall on me,
Providence has an immense *parapluie* (umbrella)
to hinder or break the force of the storm—what a comfort."

Elizabeth Ann Seton (19th century, America)

WHEN VIVACIOUS YOUNG Elizabeth Bayley, the daughter of an Episcopal doctor in New York, married her beloved William Seton she could not have anticipated what lay in store for her. Five children followed and Elizabeth happily busied herself in domestic life. After a few years, William's shipping business began to fail and he fell deathly ill. In quest of a cure, they traveled to Italy with their eldest child, but the family was quarantined in a dank hold offshore where William died. His Italian business partners comforted the widow and it was through them that Elizabeth was introduced to Roman Catholicism. Returning to America, she struggled with her desire to join the Church whose eucharistic adoration so captured her heart. When she did so, most of her family shunned her. Forced to fend for herself and her children, she opened a school. Eventually she moved to Maryland and founded a community of women, the Sisters of Charity, whose main work was to be the education of young girls, both those who were well-to-do and those who were poor. Life was hard for the fledgling community. Many died, including two of her daughters, and the efforts of administration were burdensome. Elizabeth Ann Seton suffered greatly, yet with gracefulness and courage she faced the difficulties of her life trusting that, even in hardship, God's grace was somehow to be found.

## Encountering Wisdom for Life

WHEN, IN THE DIM LIGHT of the first Easter morning, the grieving women came to the tomb to anoint Jesus' body with spices, they came with broken hearts. Not only had the one they loved died, but the radical vision of the reign of God he had shared with them seemed crushed as well. As they had agonized with him as he hung from the cross, so their dearest hope had died with his last breath. When they lay down their spice jars in the mist of morning and, to their astonishment, found the heavy stone that closed the tomb rolled away, they could not know that over the course of the next weeks and months, they, with the other disciples, would slowly come to grasp the truth of what had happened.

They would catch glimpses of their lost Lord, present to them in a new way. They would gradually begin to comprehend that an unimagined newness, the power of a love that conquered death, was now theirs. They could not yet dream that Jesus' followers, huddled together in an upper room, would receive the Holy Spirit to animate the new life they were to live. Gazing into the darkened, empty tomb, the women were only beginning to encounter the depth of the Paschal Mystery.

Right at the heart of the Christian faith is this Paschal Mystery: the profound mystery of suffering, death, and transformation whose pattern is found in Jesus' death and resurrection and which we observe during the church year as Good Friday, Easter Sunday, the forty days leading up to the Ascension, the Ascension, and Pentecost. Just as we Christians are called to participate in the Incarnation so we are also invited to share in the profound truths of the paschal cycle.

This sharing is not morbid or gloomy. Paschal death is not the sort of death that ends life and its possibilities. Paschal death is the kind of dying that, while ending something, also opens the person undergoing it to receive a richer form of life. The new life received is not merely resuscitated life (the former life brought back), but a radical new life infused with a new spirit. The Spirit that we receive, our own Pentecost born out of our participation in the paschal cycle, is not a generic Spirit. It is rather a particular gift from God, given to animate us in the particular circumstances in which we find ourselves.

**Elizabeth Seton and the Paschal Mystery.** We can see the process of the Paschal Mystery in a dramatic form at several points in Elizabeth Seton's life story. Everything in her early life had prepared Elizabeth for the contentment of marriage and motherhood. She gloried in her domestic role. Following we see how her life is so connected to the Paschal Mystery.

✠ **Death.** When the family fortunes foundered and her husband William died, her anguish was terrible. Her former life and the spirit that governed it died. Yet Elizabeth trusted that even in this dark passage, God was beckoning her. She sensed that beckoning presence on the altars of the Roman Catholic Church.

✠ **Resurrection.** Through her conversion, Elizabeth sensed that new life was offered her. Yet because of her conversion, Elizabeth's family withdrew their support.

✠ **Ascension.** Soon she had to learn a whole new way of being to support herself and her children: she began teaching school. She let go of the past, grieved her native New York, and moved to Maryland.

✠ **Pentecost.** There she was given a new spirit for an entirely new life. Under the direction of the Sulpician Fathers, she founded a religious community of women and began the process of shaping their unique common life and the work they would do. In the distinctive early American context, even Catholic Religious life had to be reinvented.

None of this was easy or straightforward. Like the women at the tomb on Easter morning, the young Elizabeth could never have imagined the future or the mystery of rising and the inspiring spirit that would be offered her. She had, however, one hope that sustained her, contained in a short phrase that she would share with others: "Run to meet your grace," she would say. In all of it, God's presence can be trusted, whether you can understand it at the time or not. The Paschal Mystery beckons us to move from life to fuller life.

The living Spirit of God is at work in the world today. The Spirit, given to the disciples at the time of Pentecost, continues to draw us together and infuse us with life. Perhaps when we think of the cross and the empty tomb as they relate to our own lives, we think mainly of "going to heaven" or of the dramatic and possibly crucifying events we might be forced to suffer. But the focus of this session is not on these types of events. Rather it is on the more ordinary ways in which, by simply being human, we either embrace or refuse the transformative power of the Paschal Mystery in the course of our lives.

Ronald Rolheiser, in *The Holy Longing*, offers us this thought: there are many little deaths we are offered and, in embracing and grieving them, we can be blessed by them and move on to a new, fuller life. Rolheiser names five of these ordinary deaths that come to each of us at one time or another: the death of our youth; our wholeness; our dreams; our honeymoons; and our ideas about Church and God.

**The Death of Our Youth.** In a culture that lionizes youth, growing old is not something most of us look forward to. Yet, the gifts of aging are real. We cannot realize them, however, if we refuse to let go of our youths or former lives. This does not mean we become grim or inflexible or boring. But having a "youthful spirit" is not the same as denying we are adults or presenting the world with a cosmetically-altered face.

As we move from childhood and adolescence to young adulthood, we need to give up infantile ways, to take responsibility for ourselves and our world. As we age, we need to embrace this new moment and be open to its wisdom. If we do, paschally,

Good Friday will have happened to us, as will the Resurrection: we will have received the new life of a twenty- or a forty- or a sixty- or an eighty-year old, a richer, fuller life than the one we had before.

**The Death of Our Wholeness.** Perhaps in our past, we have been wounded or scarred in some painful manner. Maybe we spent our childhoods being the butt of jokes because we were different from other children—we spoke another language or belonged to a foreign culture, or were not regarded as pretty or slim or athletic or smart. Perhaps as children or as adults someone betrayed or violated us, or someone dear to us. Maybe we have lost some critical capacity due to accident or disease. Failure may have derailed us. Whatever the cause we may feel as though we have lost some part of ourselves: our wholeness has died.

Without minimizing or trivializing the seriousness of our loss—all sorts of healing interventions may be needed—still, God's invitation to new life is discovered even in the most dire loss. Paschally, we are invited into the Ascension: we must grieve what has in fact died, and when the time is ripe, let it go. Let it ascend so we can receive a new spirit, not one that denies our violation or our wounds, but one that has gathered up our hard-won wisdom and lives now a new life.

**The Death of Our Dreams.** When we are young most of us imagine our future selves in rosy hues. We may have even had a shot at realizing our dreams of being a competitive athlete, a well-regarded civic leader, a noted writer, painter, or musician, the content mother of many healthy, well-adjusted children, or a successful businessperson. We may have formed a relationship with someone we hoped would be our life companion or at least seemed to be the man or woman of our dreams but ended up disappointing us.

We may find ourselves mired in regret or resentment that it didn't turn out the way we had planned. Broken dreams, broken promises, broken hearts: these are all painful parts of the human experience. It is right to mourn what will never be. But mourning is not continual. It is a paschal process that frees us to enter courageously and joyfully—like the disciples breathing in the Spirit at Pentecost—into what our lives have become; to savor the sometimes simple delights we might miss if we are mired in resentment, bitterness, and regret. There is always an offer of a new hope and God-grounded dream.

**The Death of Our Honeymoons.** However, the glow of any beginning, as wonderful as it is, does not last. Our lives change; routine sets in; we are not on vacation any more; we are no longer a high school or a college student getting ready for our lives. We are suddenly earning our way. Any marriage, friendship, collegial or work relationship, or family bond has deeply embedded within it the dynamics of the paschal cycle.

As we constantly name the relational deaths we undergo, claim the new relational phases given us, grieve what has died, and then receive a new spirit for the relationship, we plumb the depths of the central mystery of our faith. We die and rise again with a new spirit. Our Pentecost may then consist of a new adult appreciation of and expectations about our marriage partner, our colleagues, or our friendships.

**The Death of Our Ideas about Church and God.** The claims of religion open our hearts to such wonderful possibilities of hope, faith, and love. Yet in our Church communities we often find ourselves face-to-face with pettiness, conflict, unfairness, or even bigotry. One of the great tasks of spirituality is to simultaneously hang on to the beautiful vision we are offered, all the while struggling with the imperfect realization of that vision in our Church. Perhaps we try to cling to the idealized Church of the past or are so angry at the Church that we become immobilized. Either way, if we accept the Paschal Mystery, we will let ourselves grieve the past, let go of it, and be open to what is newly emerging.

Even more profoundly, we often find ourselves growing out of or changing our ideas about who God is and how God operates. Some of this is simply natural maturation. As children we hold childish, often self-centered concepts of God. Or, perhaps, we naively assume if we "follow all the rules" God will immunize us from the suffering that is part of the human condition. When suffering comes, we may feel as though God has "disappeared." But the Paschal Mystery invites us to something new. It invites us, as the grieving disciples in the Upper Room were invited, to await together the gift of the vitalizing breath of God.

It is especially in the community of Christians that this gift is discovered. God sends the Holy Spirit to each of us individually but even more, to us together. That is what Church is ultimately about: the community of Christians animated by the living Spirit, the Spirit of Truth, to be the Body of Christ in the world.

Each of these ordinary deaths, both individual and communal, is an invitation to enter into the Paschal Mystery. We must let what is dying die. We must mourn its passing in order to be open to what is to come. But we must also remember that simply letting go is not enough. We must let our deaths bless us. Whether we let go of a positive or negative past, it is *our* past. It is what brings us to this precious point in our lives where God's transforming power beckons us to become new people of the Spirit. We must remember that these deaths are not simply endings; they are beginnings as well. They are the prelude to new life and a new spirit, to the life of Easter and Pentecost. We now live in the age of the Holy Spirit, guiding and animating the living Body of Christ.

## Sharing Our Faith

✠ What new insights struck me regarding Christ's Paschal Mystery?

✠ Which of the "deaths" Rolheiser names—youth, wholeness, dreams, honeymoon, Church, and God—have I encountered? In what ways have I refused to mourn and have instead clung to or been frozen in a death that refuses to die?

✠ In our scripture passage (John 12:24) we reflected on the cycle of the life of the seed. What new life have I received from the letting go and dying to something? In what ways am I now being challenged?

## Living the Good News

*Choose how you feel the Word of God and your sharing challenge you to action for the week ahead. The best actions are always the ones that emerge from the specific contexts of your own lives and sharing. These suggested actions are just that, suggestions. If they capture your imagination and seem like the right action for your group or yourself, then proceed with one of them. If they do not, devise more appropriate individual and/or group actions.*

🌐 Determine ways in which you will surrender to God's will and welcome the enabling power of the Holy Spirit to embrace the next stage of your life.

🌐 If you find yourself unable to move forward in life because of some deep violation to you or your family, seek out a pastoral counselor to help you with this. You can ask at your local parish or call the offices of your diocese.

Bring to mind someone close to you who is experiencing hardship at this time. What are some ways you can accompany him or her to "new life"? Act on something you feel called to do for or with him or her.

Talk to someone who is a wisdom figure for you. Dialogue about the ways he or she has dealt with times of transition.

Be a support to persons who are struggling to break free from a "death" situation by volunteering your time with a social service program such as a food pantry, clinic, outreach center, etc.

Draw a picture or, using photos from magazines, create a collage that illustrates the sort of "dying" you are called to do in your life right now. Pray with this image. You might want to share these images in your group.

Given where I am in my own life and as a response to the Word of God and our sharing, I feel called to

_____

_____

## Closing Prayer

*Engage in the following ritual together.*

*You will need two large bowls, a Bible, some symbol of the Resurrection (a flower, a cross, a drawing of an empty tomb, a stone for the one that was rolled away), as well as two pieces of paper, a pencil or pen, and some wrapping paper cut into pieces. The two bowls should be in the middle, either on a table or on the floor.*

*Sit quietly for a minute to begin this ritual.*

*Invite one person to read aloud* John 12:24. *(silence)*

*Ask each person to take one sheet of writing paper and one piece of gift paper and write a word or phrase that speaks about a "death" experience in his or her life (job loss, end of relationship, resentment).*

*Pass around one of the bowls. As people drop their piece of paper in the bowl, each person says, "With the grace of God, I ask to let go of this death in my life."*

*When everyone has placed a paper in the bowl, pass around the bowl a second time, asking each person to place a piece of gift wrap in the bowl. The leader then says,*
The gift paper symbolizes God's grace
—a "free and undeserved help"*
—transforming "our many deaths."

*Catechism of the Catholic Church, (1996)

*Give each person a second sheet of paper and ask him or her to write a word or phrase that captures a gift of joy or resurrection or new life (friendship, reconciliation, a new beginning).*

*Place it in the bowl saying,*
In gratitude, I thank God for this new life.

*When all have finished, place the white cloth or cross over the sheets of paper as a symbol of resurrection.*

*Invite a second person to read* John 12:24.

*Close with a song of new life, e.g.,* "Heal Me, Lord."

*The leader then leads the others in prayer:*

Gracious God and Father,
you have shown us that paschal dying
is not the end, but the entryway
into vibrant, Spirit-filled life.
Help us to mourn what must die,
to wait for the passing of all we must release,
to wait in joy-filled anticipation
of the newness you will send.
Amen.

Leader: *Let us offer each other a sign of peace.*

## Looking Ahead

*If immediately continuing for another six weeks, prepare at home for your next session by prayerfully reading and studying Session 7. If your group is not planning to meet immediately following this first six weeks, keep in touch by phone, e-mail, or by having a family social where members of each family can enjoy food and fun together.*

## Informal Gathering

## Suggestions for Further Reading

Henri Nouwen, *Turn My Mourning into Dancing:*
*Finding Hope in Hard Times,*
W Publishing Group, a Division of Thomas Nelson, Inc.

Judith Metz, S.C., *A Retreat with Elizabeth Seton:*
*Meeting Our Grace,* A Retreat With Series,
St. Anthony Messenger Press

Sue Monk Kidd, *When the Heart Waits:*
*Spiritual Direction for Life's Sacred Questions,*
HarperCollins

*United States Catholic Catechism for Adults:*
Chapter 8. The Saving Death and Resurrection of Christ;
Chapter 9. Receive the Holy Spirit

*Catechism of the Catholic Church:*
Paragraphs 793-794, 1067-1068, 1681-1683, 2012-2016

# In My House There Are Many Rooms

## Being a Part of Church Community

## Sharing

*Briefly share on one of the following questions:*

"How am I right now?" or
"What good news would I like to share?"

## Lifting Our Hearts ...

### ... in Song

*Play or sing one of the following or another song of your choice:*

"For Living, For Dying"
"Song of the Body of Christ" / "Canción del Cuerpo de Christo"

### ... in the Quiet

*Pause for a few moments of silence and enter more deeply into the presence of God.*

### ... in the Word

*Read aloud* John 14:1-3.

*Take a few minutes to ponder a word, a phrase, a question, or a feeling that rises up in you. Reflect on this quietly; then share it aloud.*

*(Even if no one wishes to reflect aloud, permit sufficient time for silent reflection.)*

## ... in Prayer

*Conclude with this prayer spoken together:*

Gracious God and loving Father,
you invite us to trust you
and the community to whom you have given your Word.
May we become more gracious, just as you are gracious.
May we learn to accept the vast diversity of those
you call your own, just as you do.
May our hearts not be troubled
    but, as we grow in wisdom,
may we find peace in you and with each other.
We pray in Jesus' name
and through the power of the Holy Spirit.
Amen.

## Our Companion on the Journey

# St. John Bosco

"It is necessary for Christians to unite in the doing
of good works....
We Christians ought to be united in these difficult times
to promote the spirit of prayer and of charity
with the means which religion furnishes
and so remove ... those evils
which jeopardize the good morals of growing youth
in whose hands rests the destiny of civil society."

St. John Bosco (19th century, Piedmont, Italy)

JOHN (DON) BOSCO had a special love for youth, especially the Italian street children who had become so numerous in the social upheavals of the Industrial Revolution. He was from a peasant family and it became his life's work to labor tirelessly on behalf of these marginalized little ones. Convinced that all children, no matter how abused or hardened, could grow in virtue if drawn by gentleness and joy, he established the Salesians of Don Bosco who ran the Festive Oratory, a place for young people where academic and practical education and religious formation took place and where games and festivals punctuated each day. Bosco felt that priests, women religious, and lay people should form one community to minister to the young. Church law at the time didn't allow for this, so separate but affiliated groups, together known as the Salesian family, were formed. John's collaborator, Marie Mazzarello, became the foundress of the Daughters of Mary, Help of Christians, and a lively lay community, the Salesian Cooperators, was established. The young people who were the focus of the family's ministry were drawn into a holistic religious vision that honored work, health, humor, friendship, and a joyful appreciation of the gift of life.

## Encountering Wisdom for Life

IT IS NOT UNCOMMON TODAY to hear people claim they are "spiritual but not religious." What they mean by this seems to be while they are drawn to things often associated with Church—prayer, meditation, a reflective, holistic life—they do not feel drawn to particular doctrines, institutions, or communities. They don't want someone else "telling them what to do," or they feel they do not need a set of rules or precise rituals to aid them in their spiritual quest. Sometimes they just find themselves annoyed with the motley group of people who seem to make up any given Church community.

Yet community is an essential part of our genuine spiritual growth. Fr. Rolheiser has likened the Church to "going on an extended family outing" with all the inconveniences and disappointing experiences that it entails. He has also given us some wise guidance about what the Church really is (rather than what we think it ought to be) and why we need the Church as much as the Church needs us. His reflections fall under five headings: the Church as the people, as the rope, as the flawed Body, as a house with many rooms, and as a place of anointing. As you read each of these, reflect on how it relates to your own life.

**1. The Church Is the People.** Before we consider what the Church *is*, perhaps it might be best to reflect first on what the Church *is not*. The Church is *not* a group of like-minded, mutually compatible soul mates. *Neither* is it a safe refuge for a small group huddled in fear and loneliness against the evil world. *Nor* is it a family in the psychological sense, a community where we go to have all our intimate needs met. The Church *is not* made up of one roof, one ethnicity, one rulebook, one uniform book of prayer. *Nor* is it a community bound together by a shared task or one common mission. We will not always find in the Church an escape from reality or a surrogate family, or a pew full of others who all see things as we do.

Instead, the Church *is* the community gathered around the person of Christ that shares his Spirit. The word Church, *ecclesia*, means "to be called out of." We as members are called out of our varied everyday lives to belong to a People set apart. This requires that we *do* engage in some real sharing, that we pray and worship together, take responsibility for one another and are mutually accountable.

**2. The Church Is the Rope.** When we are baptized, God consecrates us. Something that is consecrated is set apart as holy. It has been claimed for some special use. So it is with us. We are tied firmly to God and God's people.

Having children generally leads parents to a maturity that draws them out of their self-centered worlds and teaches them to grow as they take responsibility for their children. When we take responsibility for our baptism, we grow up as Christians. The Church is the rope that connects us, often against our instincts, to spiritual maturity. In some sense we lose our freedom to just do what we would to squander our lives. We are chosen and as a result we are often taken where we don't want to go; we are tied to a rope that draws us fully into the life of God, and in the process, through the suffering which that entails, we gain maturity.

**3. The Church Is the Flawed Body.** We say the Church is the Body of Christ. That means *we* are the Body. But clearly, we are a flawed Body. The Christian communities in which we find ourselves—our parishes, our national and global churches—mediate God's presence to us. Through them we come to know God. But that mediation is very mixed. It is hardly perfect. While some of us would like to assume there is some perfect community somewhere, the Gospel doesn't back this up.

The disciples in all the four Gospels have a hard time "getting it." They quibble about who will be first in the kingdom, thinking of their own prestige and honor. They seem clueless when Jesus tries to teach them through parables. They fall asleep when he pleads with them to stay awake and pray with him. They deny Jesus and run away when he is persecuted and tried. The very community that is flawed is also the treasured carrier of God's presence. The Church is the flawed Body. But it is the Body.

Every age has seen itself in difficult times. Today, scandals in the Church have led some to be disillusioned and to walk away. But what is the true nature of the Church community? Was not this "mixed bag" the case with the Apostles and the original Christians? Yet, God has chosen to dwell in his imperfect Church. It has been this way—both graced and flawed—from the beginning. Perhaps we would like to think of the Church in times past in some idealized way, but neither the Gospel nor history back this up.

A glance at the life of Don Bosco will correct our view. During his lifetime the papacy was in the tumultuous process of losing its political and military role as head of the Papal States. At the same time it was the Church, mediated to the young Bosco by his pious mother and his deeply caring seminary professors, who nurtured the impoverished peasant boy in the life of faith. This was the same Church, in the form of his fellow Christians, who fiercely opposed the Oratory at the *Rifugio*, Bosco's facility for the care of street children. To his great distress, Don Bosco was obliged to give up his rooms and was subjected to obstacles, which, at times, seemed to spell the ruin of his undertaking.

His perseverance in the face of all difficulties led many to the conclusion that he was insane, and an attempt was even made to confine him in an asylum. Complaints were lodged against him, declaring his community to be a nuisance because of the character of the boys he befriended. At the same time it was the Church, in the form of his patrons and collaborators, which allowed his dreams to flourish.

Graced and flawed. There is not a saint's story that does not reflect the same struggle with community. In some eras it was not only obstacles, but also scandal which plagued the Church. Despite this human element, the Church has also faithfully proclaimed the Gospel message and has given birth to many saints.

**4. The Church Is a House with Many Rooms.** In John's Gospel (John 14:2), Jesus encourages his followers to trust in the mystery of God's love. We are told that Jesus will prepare a place for us, and that our loving Creator has prepared different places, *many* rooms or mansions. What is revealed here is the spaciousness of God's heart. That heart is broad and inclusive. God does not prepare a place just for the conservatives or the liberals or just the clergy and religious or just the laity, for men only or women only, for the young and not the old, for the black and not the white, for the educated not the uneducated, for the perfect not the imperfect. No.

As the familiar hymn text reminds us, "There is a wideness in God's mercy, like the wideness of the sea." God's heart is generous and finds a space for us with our diverse and varied lives. As God's heart is, so must ours be. We are challenged to make room in our hearts for the many different people who make up the Body of Christ.

**5. The Church Is a Place of Anointing.** Before Jesus' impending death, the Gospel of Matthew tells us, he was at the house of Simon when a woman appeared with a jar of expensive ointment with which she anointed him. When his disciples objected, Jesus told them that she did it to prepare him for his burial (Matthew 26:6-13). Anointing was what was done to a priest, prophet, and king. Jesus' unexpected kingship is prophesied in this act but, as Jesus announces, anointing was also done for the dead (see Mark 16:1).

The Church is the place where we, too, are anointed for our deaths. Paul reminds us in Romans 6 that "all of us who have been baptized into Christ Jesus were baptized into his death."

And "just as Jesus was raised from the dead ... so we too might walk in newness of life." And when we are seriously ill and near death, we can ask for the sacrament of the anointing of the sick. This sacrament "completes our identification with Jesus Christ that was begun at our Baptism. Its grace and power fortify us in our final struggles before we go to the Father's house" (*United States Catholic Catechism for Adults* p. 254).

When we come together as Church to participate in the sacraments or for other reasons, we gather to offer our love and affection, to acknowledge our shared humanity before God, to be together in community, and to offer one another the gift that the nameless woman in Matthew offered to Jesus. We must anoint one another with our love.

Don Bosco and his Salesian family knew this well when they sought to be the love of God enfleshed for the street children of Piedmont. When they took them in, schooled them both in faith and practical skills, when they arranged musical and dramatic presentations, festivals and games, they, too, were anointing each other with love.

We gather in community as Church because it is not good to be alone. We gather because we need to take our places humbly within the family of humankind, to dispel our proud fantasies about ourselves, and to carry one another's burdens. We gather to dream our deepest common dreams, and to prepare for the time when we will all be welcomed into the merciful heart of God. We discover that despite our differences, a place has been lovingly prepared.

## Sharing Our Faith

✝ What would my ideal Church community look and feel like?

✝ In what ways have I matured by being part of a Church community? Consider the joys and sufferings this has involved.

✠ There is a distinction between actions (sometimes sinful) of people in the Church and the Church's Spirit-guided proclamation of Jesus' teachings. How can I help others to see and experience the graced and flawed differences and have a better appreciation of the richness of the Church?

## Living the Good News

*Choose how you feel the Word of God and your sharing challenge you to action for the week ahead. The best actions are always the ones that emerge from the specific contexts of your own lives and sharing. These suggested actions are just that, suggestions. If they capture your imagination and seem like the right action for your group or yourself, then proceed with one of them. If they do not, devise more appropriate individual and/or group actions.*

Find out about the Church on the diocesan or statewide level. Synods, programs for theological study or pastoral training, faith-based programs that serve those who are poor, lay associate programs run by orders of religious men and women, retreat opportunities: all these and more are expressions of the Church's life.

To become more conscious of the variety of people who have become saints, choose a book on the lives of the saints or one particular saint and take time for reflective and prayerful reading.

Visit other Catholic parishes in your city or state, especially those in a region with different ethnic and cultural communities from your own. Celebrate Eucharist with them and celebrate the vast diversity, yet the profound unity of the community of which you are a part.

● If you are not already involved, seek out a group—a Bible study, parish committee, music ministry, homebound ministry, or other group—and engage in it.

● When possible, engage in ecumenical services in your area or join in service projects.

Given where I am in my own life and as a response to the Word of God and our sharing, I feel called to

_____

_____

## Closing Prayer

*You may wish to conclude this session by having one person read this reflection by the late Carlo Carretto, who in his book,* I Sought and I Found: My Experience of God and of the Church *(Orbis Books, 1984), addressed the Church in these words:*

How much I must criticize you, my church,
and yet how much I love you!
You have made me suffer more than anyone
and yet I owe more to you than anyone.
I should like to see you destroyed
yet I need your presence.
You have given me much scandal
yet you alone have made me understand holiness.
…
No, I cannot be free of you,
for I am one with you, even if not completely you.
Then too, where would I go?
To build another church?

But I could not build one without the same defects,
for they are my defects.
And again, if I were to build another church,
it would be my church, not Christ's church.
No, I am old enough, I know better.

*Close by praying together:*

May God the Father's heart be ours.
May Jesus our brother's love be ours.
May the Spirit's radiant wisdom be ours. Amen.

## Looking Ahead

*Prepare at home for your next session by prayerfully reading
and studying Session 8.*

## Informal Gathering

## SUGGESTIONS FOR FURTHER READING

Michael Leach and Therese J. Borchard, *I Like Being Catholic:*
*Treasured Traditions, Rituals, and Stories,*
Doubleday

Michael Downey, *Altogether Gift:*
*A Trinitarian Spirituality,*
Orbis Books

Carlo Carretto, *The God Who Comes* or *I Sought and I Found:*
*My Experience of God and of the Church,*
Orbis Books

Robert Schiele, *Fifteen Days of Prayer with Don Bosco,*
Fifteen Days of Prayer Series,
Liguori Publications

Penelope J. Ryan, Ph.D., *Practicing Catholic:*
*The Search for a Livable Catholicism,*
Henry Holt & Company

*United States Catholic Catechism for Adults:*
Chapter 10. The Church: Reflecting the Light of Christ;
Chapter 11. The Four Marks of the Church

*Catechism of the Catholic Church:*
Paragraphs 751-752, 770-771, 776-779, 787-796,
805-810, 872-873, 953

# Eucharist

## God's Gift and
## Our Response

## Sharing

*Briefly share on one of the following questions:*

"How am I right now?" or
"What good news would I like to share?"

## Sharing the Good News

*Share how you did with your action response from the last session
(Living the Good News) or how you were able to incorporate the
message of the last session into your daily lives.*

## Lifting Our Hearts ...

### ... in Song

*Play or sing one of the following or another song of your choice:*

"We Come to Your Feast"
"Pan de Vida"

### ... in the Quiet

*Pause for a few moments of silence and enter more deeply into
the presence of God.*

### ... in the Word

*Read aloud* 1 Corinthians 11:23-26.

*Take a few minutes to ponder a word, a phrase, a question, or a feeling that rises up in you. Reflect on this quietly; then share it aloud.*

*(Even if no one wishes to reflect aloud, permit sufficient time for silent reflection.)*

### ... in Prayer

*Conclude with this prayer spoken together:*

> Gracious God, in Jesus the Christ
> you have given us birth
> and continue to sustain us in our new life.
> May the Eucharist be the source
> of our courage and our hope.
> Through our intimate sharing in your life,
> may your desire for this world become ours.
> Amen.

## Our Companion on the Journey

# Archbishop Oscar Romero

"The Eucharist makes us look back to Calvary
twenty centuries ago
and beyond that to Moses and the old covenant,
an incomparable horizon of history.
But it also looks ahead to the future,
to the eternal, eschatological, and definitive horizon
that presents itself as a demanding ideal to all political systems,
to all social struggles, to all those concerned
for the earth."

Archbishop Oscar Romero (20th century, Central America)

A T 6:30 ON THE EVENING of March 24, 1980,
Oscar Romero, Archbishop of San Salvador,
was saying Mass before the altar of the small
chapel of the hospital of Divine Providence. Just
as he was about to elevate the bread and wine for
the sacrifice he was felled by an assassin's bullet.
A beloved pastor of his Salvadoran people, Romero
was born in 1917. He trained in theology in Rome,
was ordained and began what was later seen as
a brilliant career in his native country. When he
was appointed archbishop in 1977, El Salvador
was engaged in a civil war; the killing of peas-
ants was everyday news, massacres committed by
military and paramilitary organizations terror-
ized the populace. Although originally thought of
as a non-controversial choice, Romero soon felt
his Christian conscience left him no choice but to
speak out. When two of his priests were murdered
because they spoke out for the poor, he set up a
permanent commission for the defense of human
rights. Meanwhile crowds began flocking to his
Masses. Not everyone agreed with Romero's defense of the poor and his criticism of a government
that slaughtered its own citizens. But his deep spirituality, centered on the eucharistic heart of Jesus,
led him to proclaim, "When the church hears the
cry of the oppressed it cannot but denounce the
social structures that give rise to and perpetuate
the misery from which the cry arises." As he grew
in serenity and patience, nurtured by the Eucharist, he made the increasingly difficult sacrifices
that God would require of him, accepting even the
violent death that he foresaw would be his.

## Encountering Wisdom for Life

A T THE HEART OF OUR Catholic Christian faith is the Sunday celebration of the Eucharist, also traditionally known as the Holy Sacrifice of the Mass. The liturgical action of the Eucharist binds and bonds us in deep union with Christ and with the eucharistic community, which is both the people present and the entire communion of saints.

In his first encyclical (Christmas 2005), Pope Benedict XVI underlines this doubled meaning of "communion."

> Union with Christ is also union with all those to whom he gives himself. I cannot possess Christ just for myself; I can belong to him only in union with all those who have become, or who will become, his own. Communion draws me out of myself towards him, and thus also towards unity with all Christians. We become "one body," completely joined in a single existence.
>
> *Deus Caritas Est,* 14

We are a eucharistic people: we are nurtured and transformed by our intimate contact with Christ in the sacrament of the altar. This true presence is a mystery that can, and should, urge us to reverence. The traditional devotional practices of benediction and adoration developed to give expression to this reverence. It is extremely important there also be a dynamic, transforming dimension to our being a eucharistic people. Father Ron Rolheiser opens up for us dimensions of the mystery of the real presence as he reflects on the themes of a) the Eucharist as touch and b) the Eucharist as taking us from self-protection to being food for the life of the world.

**The Eucharist as Touch.** In an essay entitled "In Praise of Skin," author Brenda Peterson tells how at one point in her life she was afflicted by terrible skin rashes. Every medication and treatment she tried failed to heal her. One day her grandmother assessed her and pronounced, "Skin needs to be touched." Her grandmother then gave her regular skin massages and these did what all the sophisticated treatments couldn't: they cured her. Peterson's grandmother was right: skin needs to be touched in ways that honor and affirm that we are embodied persons. God knows that better than anyone. That's why we have the Eucharist. Through it, skin gets touched.

The Eucharist is not an abstraction, a theological creed, a philosophy, or a moral precept. It is a bodily embrace, something astoundingly physical, a real encounter with Jesus Christ. It is true that we tend today to be shy of this kind of talk, to think about communion as something disembodied and symbolic. But Christianity is the most earthy of religions. It does not call us out of the physical, out of the world, or out of the body. Rather, Christ enters the physical, becomes one with it, blesses it, redeems it, and tells us there is no reason to escape from it. The claim of eating Christ's flesh and blood (John 6:53-62) even troubled Jesus' contemporaries: "This teaching is difficult; who can accept it?" (John 6:60) the crowds said in the Gospel of John. As astonishing as this claim is, it is wonderful. In the Eucharist, our skin gets touched. And, like the woman with the skin rash, we need to be touched. We need to be touched in order to be healed. We need to be touched to live.

The late essayist André Dubus once wrote about why he went to daily Eucharist, even though most of his literary colleagues found the practice odd. He wrote,

> I received the sacrament I still believe in … the priest
> elevated the host, then the chalice, and spoke the words

of the ritual, and the bread became flesh, the wine became blood, and minutes later I placed on my tongue the taste of forgiveness and of love that affirmed, perhaps celebrated, my being alive, my being mortal.... This has to do with mortality and the touch of flesh, and my belief in the sacrament of the Eucharist is simple: without touch, God is a monologue, an idea, a philosophy: he must touch and be touched....

Of course, one of the tests as to how we are touched by the Eucharist is how we then reach out to touch others. As Pope Benedict XVI says in his encyclical on Christian love,

... Eucharistic communion includes the reality both of being loved and of loving others in turn. A Eucharist which does not pass over into the concrete practice of love is intrinsically fragmented.

*Deus Caritas Est,* 14

**Eucharist as Food for the Life of the World.** Not only do we tend to "spiritualize" the Eucharist, we also tend to privatize it. While it is true that the encounter with Christ in the Eucharist is intimate and personal, it is not an encounter that is meant for us alone. Jesus himself did not come into the world to be concerned only with himself: his personal plans, his fulfillment, his safety. In defining his meaning and ministry, he asserted, "[T]he bread that I will give for the life of the world is my flesh" (John 6:51). We can easily miss what is really contained in that statement.

Notice what he is *not* saying: Jesus is not saying that his flesh is food for the life of the Church or for the life of Christians or for the life of the deserving and righteous. Albeit that believers get fed, and often fed first, but the ultimate reason why Jesus came was not simply to feed us. His body is food for the life of the world and the world is bigger than any of us and bigger than the Church. Jesus came into the world to nourish it. He was born in a manger—a feeding trough where animals come to eat—and he ends up on a table, an altar, to feed human beings who in turn feed one another. Jesus came as nourishment for the planet.

We are called, like Jesus, to be food for the life of the world. As Cardinal Basil Hume once put it, our real reason to be is beyond our own lives. That does not mean the Church should not have an internal agenda. In order to be a body that can provide nourishment, the Church legitimately needs to generate, foster, and encourage its own life. Church life exists to build up a body, but that body exists not simply for itself.

Our task—and this is something we as individual Christians, not just those responsible for the governance of the Church, must take seriously—is not to defend ourselves or even carve out some peace for ourselves against a world that sometimes prefers not to have us around. Our real reason for being here is to share our very life with the world. This is what it means to be a eucharistic people.

Oscar Romero certainly knew that truth. It was a truth he did not fully grasp until he began his pastoral ministry as Archbishop of San Salvador and gradually became aware of the full extent of human rights abuses perpetrated against those who were oppressed in his country. For him, there could be no political justification and no national security concerns that could justify such horrifying treatment and murder of God's children. For him, the mystery of Jesus' dying and rising was taking place in the agony and liberation of those who were poor.

For the Salvadoran archbishop, the Eucharist was not only food to sustain the hard journey, presence to accompany him on the path, but also the guiding vision and the path itself. Romero shared in the passion of Jesus and like him, gave his life for a transformed, kingdom-centered world. His witness continues to feed us today.

## Sharing Our Faith

✚ Reflect on the role the Eucharist has played in your own faith journey. Share what Eucharist means to you.

✚ In what ways does the theme of touch—God's touching us, we touching God—move me? Share your thoughts.

✚ Oscar Romero's life shows us the Eucharist in action. What other saints or people alive today show us we are called to be food for the life of the world? Celebrate the witness of these eucharistic people by sharing a story.

✚ The Eucharist invites us to be bread, leaven for the life of the world. Decide how you might, as individuals or as a group, be bread for the world.

## Living the Good News

*Choose how you feel the Word of God and your sharing challenge you to action for the week ahead. The best actions are always the ones that emerge from the specific contexts of your own lives and sharing. These suggested actions are just that, suggestions. If they capture your imagination and seem like the right action for your group or yourself, then proceed with one of them. If they do not, devise more appropriate individual and/or group actions.*

Prepare for Communion next Sunday by reflecting on the reverence due to God who comes to us as food and drink and the familiar, intimate response that such a familiar, intimate gesture as tasting and eating calls forth. Dare to believe that the Eucharist is a genuine encounter with God who loves and cherishes you.

Speak out on behalf of ending hunger. Contact and become involved with your local food bank or one of the following:

### Bread for the World

50 F Street, NW
Suite 500
Washington, DC 20001

| | |
|---|---|
| *Phone:* | 800-82-BREAD or 202-639-9400 |
| *Fax:* | 202-639-9401 |
| *Website:* | www.bread.org |
| *Email:* | bread@bread.org |

### Catholic Relief Services

228 West Lexington Street
Baltimore, MD 21201-3413

| | |
|---|---|
| *Phone:* | 888-277-7575 Mon.-Fri., 9 AM-5 PM, EST or 800-736-3467 after hours & weekends, EST |
| *Website:* | www.crs.org |
| *Email:* | info@crs.org |

### Catholic Campaign for Human Development (CCHD)

3211 Fourth Street, NE
Washington, DC 20017-1194

| | |
|---|---|
| *Phone:* | 202-541-3000 @ USCCB |
| *Voice:* | 202-541-3210 |
| *Fax:* | 202-541-3329 |
| *Email:* | cchdpromo@usccb.org |
| *Websites:* | www.nccbuscc.org/cchd/contact.shtml www.usccb.org/cchd/povertyusa/index.htm |

Read more about the Eucharist in the *Catechism of the Catholic Church* (1322-1419). Share some of your insights with a friend.

As well as being the continuing sacrifice of Jesus on the altar, the communion table is a banquet table to which we are invited. In this sense it is a foretaste of the banquet that will take place when God will establish his kingdom in its fullness. Draw a picture or write a description of what you think the fullness of God's kingdom and a celebratory banquet there might look like. Who is present? What happens? Give thanks for this hope.

Spend some time before the Blessed Sacrament thanking Christ for the gift of Eucharist and asking him to help you be bread for others.

Given where I am in my own life and as a response to the Word of God and our sharing, I feel called to

_____

_____

## Closing Prayer

*Share prayers of intercession, petition, or praise.*

*Pray together the Lord's Prayer.*
*Then conclude with the adaptation of a prayer written by Oscar Romero for a Lenten retreat he made in 1980.*

> I want to be with Jesus and share in his obedience to God's saving plan.

> I beg pardon of God for the human impediments in my performance as his instrument.

I want to be joined more closely to God's will.

I ask God to make his love, justice, and truth shine through me more easily ...

I fear because of the weakness of my flesh,

but I pray the Lord to give me serenity and perseverance ...

Amen.

## Looking Ahead

*Prepare at home for your next session by prayerfully reading and studying Session 9.*

## Informal Gathering

## SUGGESTIONS FOR FURTHER READING

Stephen B. Clark, *Catholics and the Eucharist:*
*A Scriptural Introduction,*
Charis Books

Henri Nouwen, *With Burning Hearts:*
*A Meditation on the Eucharistic Life,*
Orbis Books

*Oscar Romero: Reflections on His Life and Writings,*
Modern Spiritual Masters Series,
edited by Marie Dennis, Renny Golden, Scott Wright,
Orbis Books

Judith M. Noone, MM, *The Same Fate as the Poor,*
Orbis Books

*United States Catholic Catechism for Adults:*
Chapter 17. The Eucharist:
Source and Summit of the Christian Life.

*Catechism of the Catholic Church:*
Paragraphs 1322-1419

# Walk Justly

## Sharing

*Briefly share on one of the following questions:*

"How am I right now?" or
"What good news would I like to share?"

## Sharing the Good News

*Share how you did with your action response from the last session (Living the Good News) or how you were able to incorporate the message of the last session into your daily lives.*

## Lifting Our Hearts ...

### ... in Song

*Play or sing one of the following or another song of your choice:*

"This Is" (Song of Micah)
"We Are Called"

### ... in the Quiet

*Pause for a few moments of silence and enter more deeply into the presence of God.*

## ... in the Word

*Read aloud* Micah 6:8

*Take a few minutes to ponder a word, a phrase, a question, or a feeling that rises up in you. Reflect on this quietly; then share it aloud.*

*(Even if no one wishes to reflect aloud, permit sufficient time for silent reflection.)*

## ... in Prayer

*Conclude with this prayer spoken together:*

> Creator God and loving Father,
> you give us life at every moment.
> We ask you for so many things.
> May we be still and quiet enough
> to attend to what *you* ask of us:
> To act justly, to love tenderly,
> and to walk humbly with you.*
> We ask this through Jesus and the Holy Spirit
> who dwell in love with you for ever.
> Amen.
>
> * Micah 6:8

## Our Companion on the Journey

# Blessed Damien of Molokai

"On May 11, 1873, the steamer Kilauea deposited thirty-three-year-old Father Joseph Damien de Veuster on the landing at Molokai Island. The attending Bishop told the disease-ridden crowd from the leper colony gathered there that he had brought them a priest, "one who will be a father to you, and who loves you so much that ... he does not hesitate to become one of you; to live and die with you."

Bishop Maigret of Father Damien of Molokai
(Hawaiian Islands, 19th century)

A BELGIAN MISSIONARY of the Congregation of the Sacred Hearts of Jesus and Mary, Damien de Veuster was sent to the Hawaiian Islands to minister to the native population. For nine years he brought his enthusiasm and energy to the task, preaching the Gospel, building chapels, and helping the people farm on the main island of Hawaii. In 1873 he visited the smaller island of Molokai, a bare hellish place that had been set aside as a leper colony. The disease, called the "separating sickness," was greatly feared and people in the colony were isolated from other human contact in squalid conditions and were visited by a priest only once a year. Seeing the misery of these demoralized, shunned, and suffering human beings, Damien volunteered to stay with them. He lived among them for fifteen years, attending to every possible spiritual and physical need: he cleaned wounds, built houses, organized feasts, processions, choirs and musical groups, dug graves, administered the sacraments, and presided at funerals. His advocacy for better conditions for these forgotten ones was impassioned and sometimes brought him into conflict with those who thought him a fool. But through his persistence, those in authority were moved to change their policies, and conditions on Molokai changed for the better. Fr. Damien eventually contracted leprosy himself and died among the least of the least whom he had come to know as his dearest friends.

## Encountering Wisdom for Life

W HAT IS IT ABOUT Damien's story that inspires us? What sparks our imagination and recognizes holiness in his actions? That is the holy energy of Damien, and it represents what God can do to one's holy desires in a way that brings contemplation/prayer and action/justice together to touch the world with God's grace in a particular moment and place.

It is a common misconception that the spiritual life and working for justice and peace are two separate enterprises. Contemplation and action, sometimes imaged in the biblical sisters Mary (who sat rapt at the Lord's feet) and Martha (who scurried about doing the housework), have, in fact, often been contrasted. Despite this, our long tradition rooted in Scripture convinces us that the two cannot be divorced. The Book of Genesis lays the foundation for this assertion. It affirms that God made all people equal in dignity, that the earth and everything in it belongs to everyone equally, that all human beings are co-responsible with God in helping to protect the dignity of all, and that the physical earth itself needs to be respected.

All the prophets, in their different ways, attest to one truth: the quality of our faith is measured by the justice found in our society, and that justice is to be measured by how we treat those with the least status. Jesus affirms this. He tells us that our relationship with God is intimately connected to our relationship with the weakest members of society. Over and over the Gospels show him standing with those who are outcasts, poor, and marginalized. He teaches us that, in the end, when we stand before God, we will be asked about the hungry, the impoverished, the sick and imprisoned and what we did for them. "Truly I tell you, just as you did it to one of the least of these, who are members of my family, you did it to me ... just as you did not do it to one of the least of these, you did not do it to me (Matthew 25:40, 45).

**Justice Is More than Charity.** Few of us would intentionally turn our backs on those in need. Most of us give to the Sunday collection and support charitable causes, all of which is good. But what Jesus and the prophets were talking about was not simply charity. They were also talking about justice. *The distinction is important.*

A short parable may help to explain the difference. Once there was a town built beyond the bend in a river. One day, some children noticed three bodies floating in the river, one was dead, one was sick, and one was a healthy child. They rushed to tell the adults who buried the dead, brought the sick one to a hospital, and found a family to care for the child. This went on repeatedly for years and the good townsfolk would duly take care of those who floated down river to them. Over time, they developed efficient and elaborate systems of care and took pride in their generosity. However, during all these years, nobody thought to go up the river beyond the bend and discover why all these wounded bodies came floating down.

This parable speaks of the difference between charity and justice. Charity simply tends to the injured. Social justice tries to go up the river to find out why there are injured, and then tries to change the situation that created the river of homeless, wounded, and dead bodies in the first place.

What is implied in this is a radical change in the way things are done. Justice requires that the world be organized so as to create a playing field in which all can participate with dignity. No small task. But that is what distinguishes it from charity, which while providing needed relief from suffering, does not address the deeper causes of suffering. For a Christian, engagement in such radical change is not first and foremost a question of politics and economics, although these may be involved. Rather, the prime motivation for seeking to change the world must be the furtherance of the ideal of the kingdom Jesus proclaimed—a kingdom of joy and peace for all. Our Catholic tradition offers us a rich heritage for thinking and acting justly. It requires that we learn to think about morality not simply in personal terms, but in communal terms. To lead truly Christian lives we must not only be personally moral, we must be sure that the institutions and structures we live with are just, that they protect and allow for the flourishing of the most vulnerable in society, the lepers of our own day, as it were.

Benedict XVI reminds us that the Church

> ... cannot and must not remain on the sidelines in the fight for justice. She has to play her part through rational argument and she has to reawaken the spiritual energy without which justice, which always demands sacrifice, cannot prevail and prosper.

*Deus Caritas Est,* 28a

**Catholic Social Teaching.** There are a number of key principles of Catholic social thought that should guide all our actions and views. Here we highlight three:

✳ Each human being is created by God and gifted with an inherent dignity that is not earned by any achievement and can never be lost, even by the most inhuman behavior.

✳ Each human being realizes his or her full humanity only in community. We have a divine mandate to honor each other's intrinsic dignity and take responsibility for one another. Through our willingness or failure to do this, we either build up or destroy, bless or curse one another.

✳ We owe each other not only reverence, but all the goods and opportunities that make a dignified life possible. We owe each member of the human community a fundamental justice, which implies at least minimal participation in all aspects of life in community. Those rights are not only civil and political, but also social and economic (food, shelter, health care, education, and freedom from exploitation and violence).

Damien of Molokai serves as a powerful example of the way the Gospel imperative for justice was lived out in a concrete time and circumstance. The Church of his day certainly took seriously the cry of the poor. But lepers were, for virtually everyone, beyond the pale. The hideous, disfiguring disease was greatly feared and anyone who contracted it in Hawaii was sent away from family and friends to be hidden away on the isolated island of Molokai. So great was the fear that, until Damien came, the local Church fulfilled its pastoral obligation by sending a priest to administer sacraments only infrequently and from the safe distance of an offshore boat—no one dared to get too close.

Damien encountered these outcasts not as a threat to himself, but as fellow human beings. He felt their loneliness and despair at being cut off from ordinary human care and the nurture of the sacraments. Damien advocated vigorously to improve the terrible conditions in which they lived, so much so that civil and Church officials wearied of his constant demands for medical supplies, clean housing, and pastoral help. Eventually, because of Fr. Damien, the despised and shunned faces came to be seen for what they were—the faces of God's forgotten children.

To practice justice is to examine, challenge, and try to reform systems (economic, social, political, cultural, mythic, and religious) that unjustly penalize some even as they unjustly reward others. In this way, all God's creation will flourish in the manner God intends. Additionally, it is important that we attend to the *way* we go about seeking change on behalf of these principles.

One of the deepest mysteries of the Christian faith is that the revelation of divine love in the person of Jesus was not a love that came by violence and force. The superhero who battles evil by crushing it with fierce weapons and violent conquest is the opposite of the story of Jesus. Jesus, in fact, is the ultimate example of the nonviolent peacemaker. His approach to radical change was *not* to mimic the violence, injustice, war, egoism, and hardness of heart that he sought to transform. Instead, he chose another path. As must we. All our actions must be rooted in the power of genuine love and respect, not in self-righteous anger or a sense of moral superiority.

Our actions on behalf of justice must not seek to overcome an enemy by defeating him or her, but by inviting and winning him or her over. Only love can do that. Patience and a genuine hope in the power of God to work through us and change things is required. God's power does not overpower. It lies muted, at the deep moral and spiritual base of things. It does not overcome with muscle, or glamour, or brilliance, or speed. God's power is compassionate, understanding, and forgiving. We may not always know what strategy to take but we can always know Jesus stands with us in the midst of brokenness, among those who are poor, marginalized, and forgotten. And that his way is the way of nonviolence and peace.

## Sharing Our Faith

✠ Share examples of charity and justice in action from your own life and the lives of others. What particular needs do works of charity meet? Works of justice? What balance do I have in my life between the two?

✠ Give some thought to the three key principles of Catholic social thought mentioned above. In what ways am I challenged to rethink some of my views? For example, you might ask yourself: How have I viewed those who are poor, single parents, criminals, or people of differing ethnic, national, or racial background from my own? How will I improve my various mindsets and modify my behavior?

✝ Imagine yourself in the Garden of Gethsemane as Jesus tells his followers to put away their swords. His way is not the way of violence. Reflect on what it means to follow this surprising Lord. What changes would be required of me to follow Jesus' strong but peaceful ways?

## Living the Good News

*Choose how you feel the Word of God and your sharing challenge you to action for the week ahead. The best actions are always the ones that emerge from the specific contexts of your own lives and sharing. These suggested actions are just that, suggestions. If they capture your imagination and seem like the right action for your group or yourself, then proceed with one of them. If they do not, devise more appropriate individual and/or group actions.*

Find out about parish twinning programs (programs that twin a parish in an impoverished nation with a parish in the United States.). If your parish has such a program, become involved. If not, contact a parish that does have this program and have one of its members come give a talk on the twinning program in his or her parish and tell how it has enlivened and enriched their communal faith. For more information, contact the following:

### The Parish Twinning Program of the Americas

208 Leake Avenue
Nashville, TN 37205 U.S.A.
    *Phone:*  615-356-5999
    *Fax:*  615-352-5114
    *Website:*  www.parishprogram.org
    *Email:*  parishprogram@aol.com

Take a specific action toward changing attitudes or unfair legislation regarding those who are homeless, those without health care, those who suffer exploitation and violence, and those who are most defenseless.

Make a visit as a group to a local shelter for homeless families. Do not simply volunteer and go home, but make an appointment with the shelter coordinator to discuss the causes of homelessness in your city. Listen to the stories of the families who find themselves without a home.

Choose and become familiar with one of the social encyclicals or pastoral letters dealing with a justice issue. (See Suggestions for Further Reading.)

Learn more about what you consider to be the leprosy of today that separates us from others. Reach out this week to someone who lives on the margins.

Study the book *Living Peace* by Fr. John Dear, S.J., recommended in this chapter. If you are involved with some cause that advocates for the forgotten and despised, give some thought to the methods employed by those who advocate. Are they following the way of the nonviolent Christ? Bring the model of Jesus, the peacemaker, to your reflection. If you have questions about the means used to pursue an end, even a good end, discuss it with the organizers of the cause.

In the *Catechism of the Catholic Church,* reflect on the section on the dignity of the human person (1700-1876) and social justice (1928-1948).

Given where I am in my own life and as a response to the Word of God and our sharing, I feel called to

# Closing Prayer

In *The Holy Longing*, Fr. Rolheiser offers a justice commentary on the Lord's Prayer and it might be appropriate to pray a shortened version of it as this session closes. His commentary helps us to see the intimate connection between our daily lives, our common life in worship, and the larger life around us.

*Take turns praying each phrase of the Lord's Prayer, pausing briefly between each to reflect upon its meaning.*

*Our Father* ... who always stands with all including the weak, powerless, poor, abandoned, sick, aged, very young, unborn, and marginalized.

*Who art in heaven* ... where everything will be reversed, where the first will be last, and where all will be well and every manner of being will be well.

*Hallowed be thy name* ... may the reverence we give your name make us reverent before our neighbor's pain.

*Thy kingdom come* ... help us to create a just world where, beyond our own needs and hurts, we will do justice, love tenderly, and walk humbly with you and each other.

*Thy will be done* ... open us so that your life might flow through our veins and radiate your equal love for all and your special love for the poor.

*On earth as in heaven* ... may what we create in this world reflect your glory so that the graciousness and justice of heaven will be visible within all of our structures on earth.

*Give* ... life and love to us and help us to know that nothing comes to us by right and that we must give because we have been given to. Teach us that giving is more than casting off surplus goods and money.

*Us* ... the truly plural us. May we give not simply to our own but to everyone, including those who are very different from us.

*This day* ... not tomorrow. Do not let us procrastinate into some indefinite future so that we live in the face of injustice with all our good excuses for our inactivity.

*Our daily bread* ... so that each person in the world may have enough food, clean water, clean air, adequate health care, and sufficient access to education so as to have sustenance for a healthy life.

*And forgive us our trespasses* ... forgive us our blindness toward our neighbor, our self-preoccupation, racism, sexism, and incurable propensity to worry only about ourselves and our own.

*As we forgive those who trespass against us* ... help us to forgive, to be mellow of spirit, to not grow bitter with age, and to forgive our imperfect parents and world.

*And do not put us to the test* ... spare us your Gospel scrutiny for none of us has heard the cry of the poor with your ears. Give us, instead, more days to mend our ways, our selfishness, and our systems.

*But deliver us from evil* ... that is, from the blindness that lets us continue to participate in anonymous systems within which we need not see who gets less as who gets more.

Amen.

## Looking Ahead

*Prepare at home for your next session by prayerfully reading and studying Session 10.*

## Informal Gathering

## SUGGESTIONS FOR FURTHER READING

John Dear, *Living Peace*, Doubleday

Edward P. Deberri, James E. Hug, Peter J. Henriot, and Michael J. Schultheis, *Catholic Social Teaching: Our Best Kept Secret*, Orbis Books

Joan Guntzelman, *A Retreat With Mother Teresa and Damien of Molokai: Caring for Those Who Suffer (Hope for the Poorest of the Poor)*, A Retreat With Series, St. Anthony Messenger Press

John Paul II, *The Gospel of Life (Evangelium Vitae)*

United States Bishops, *Brothers and Sisters to Us: United States Bishops Pastoral Letter on Racism in Our Day*, United States Conference of Catholic Bishops

Bishops Committee on Black Catholics, United States Conference of Catholic Bishops, *For the Love of One Another: A Special Message on the Occasion of the Tenth Anniversary of Brothers and Sisters to Us*, United States Conference of Catholic Bishops

*United States Catholic Catechism for Adults:*
Chapter 24. Life in Christ—Part Two;
Chapter 36. Jesus Taught Us to Pray

*Catechism of the Catholic Church:*
Paragraphs 1805, 1807, 1928-42, 2425-26,2832;
The Lord's Prayer, Paragraphs 2759-2865

# Loving Well

## Spirituality and
## Sexuality

## Sharing

*Briefly share on one of the following questions:*

"How am I right now?" or
"What good news would I like to share?"

## Sharing the Good News

*Share how you did with your action response from the last session (Living the Good News) or how you were able to incorporate the message of the last session into your daily lives.*

## Lifting Our Hearts ...

### ... in Song

*Play or sing one of the following or another song of your choice:*

"We Have Been Told"
"You Are Mine"

### ... in the Quiet

*Pause for a few moments of silence and enter more deeply into the presence of God.*

## ... in the Word

*Read aloud* 1 Corinthians 13:4-8.

*Take a few minutes to ponder a word, a phrase, a question, or a feeling that rises up in you. Reflect on this quietly; then share it aloud.*

*(Even if no one wishes to reflect aloud, permit sufficient time for silent reflection.)*

## ... in Prayer

*Conclude with this prayer spoken together:*

> Creator God,
> you bless us with breath
> and fill us with the fire of love;
> May we love well.
> May our loving always bless others.
> You bless us with the capacity to create;
> may our creativity flourish.
> May what we bring to life
> become the song that captures hearts
> and the dance that leads us back to you.
> This we pray in Jesus' name
> and through the power of the Holy Spirit.
> Amen.

## Our Companion on the Journey

# Sr. Thea Bowman

> "Children of the universe,
> we come together in Jesus' name,
> and the only answer we can offer to one another
> is the love that is found in the word of God,

the love that is shared and celebrated in Jesus' name.
Love, enunciated in a thousand languages,
    a thousand symbols,
a thousand rituals, a thousand ways
so that the giftedness and the heritage of the
    multiplicity of God's people
becomes available to all of us and to the church
    that we call our home....
To what extent are you ready to eat, to pray,
to work, to play with the people of the universe?
And if you haven't got time to play with us,
to put your feet under the table
    and rest yourself a while,
it is unlikely that you can share faith,
    hope and love with us.
Jesus had time to spend at the wedding feast.
He and his disciples were there
    because it was important to be there."

Sister Thea Bowman (20th century, America)

GIFTED WITH a beautiful singing voice, a
brilliant mind, and a dynamic personality,
Bertha Bowman joined the Franciscan Sisters
of Perpetual Adoration and took the name Thea
(belongs to God). After 16 years of teaching at all
levels of school, Thea was made consultant for
multicultural awareness in the Diocese of Jackson,
Mississippi. She gave lively presentations across the
country that combined singing, story telling, Gospel
preaching, and prayer. Everything Sister Thea did
was directed toward breaking down barriers of
prejudice and hatred so that all could better understand the diversity of cultures and groups that
make up the human family.

## Encountering Wisdom for Life

SOME ANCIENT Greek philosophers (as noted in earlier sessions) used to say we are fired into life with a madness that is the root of all love, hate, creativity, sadness, and joy. A Christian might add that God, the Creator of the universe, put that power, our sexuality, within us so that we also might be creative and, like God, look upon what we have helped create and overflow with a joy that breaks the bonds of our selfishness and exclaims, "It is good!" Sexuality, understood broadly as the creative capacity within us, is at the root of the spiritual life. It is the most powerful of fires, the best of fires, yet also it could be dangerous. It is part of spiritual practice to learn how to channel this powerful fire in life-giving, not destructive, ways.

In order to thoughtfully do this, we must have an understanding of what sexuality is and is not. The word *sex* has a Latin root, the verb *secare*, which literally means, "to cut " "amputate," "sever from the whole." If, for example, you were to cut a branch from a tree, you would have "sexed" that branch. If the branch could feel, it would experience being lonely and disconnected and have a longing to be reconnected to that from which it was severed. So, too, we come into the world like severed branches fired with a longing to be reconnected.

Our ultimate longing is for God, and we long for other reconnections—we desire intimacy. We long for the protection of a parent's arms, the abiding support of the arm of friendship, the embrace of a beloved, the consolation of having a child fill our own arms, and the excitement of striking the spark of the creative imagination. We are made this way by God. We are made to be creative and our ache to be reconnected propels us into the creativity that is our great gift.

**A Creative Life-Giving Power.** Sexuality and having sex are not the same thing. Sexuality is an all-encompassing creative fire, the drive for love, communion, community, friendship, family, affection, wholeness, consummation, creativity, and self-transcendence. On the other hand, *genitality*, having sex, is only one small part of that larger reality. Genitality is also a powerful, distilled aspect of our larger creative capacity and, as such, our tradition cautions us not to trivialize or denigrate it. We should never assume that having sex is a neutral act—as part of our divinely given gift it is sacred—nor should we make the mistake of thinking that genital expression is the whole of sexuality and burden it with all the weight of our deep desires.

We are sexually healthy when we have mutually respectful love, community, family, friendship, creativity, and delight in our lives. The ancient Christian writers knew love was a reality with many interpenetrating dimensions. Love referred, at one and the same time, to a) love's playfulness and humor; b) erotic attraction: the desire to have sex; c) falling in love: romance and obsession; d) domestic, familial love; e) friendship; and f) altruistic, selfless love. Unlike frequently voiced contemporary opinions, the ancient writers did not expect one aspect of love to carry all the others.

What ties these aspects of our sexuality together is that they all are fueled by longing. They arise out of our deep sense that we are cut off and need, for our completion, to reconnect. No matter what dimension of our sexuality we consider, we must always be aware that sexuality is powerful. It changes things. It is creative. Exercised well, it makes us fruitful, whole. We bring generative energy into the world to make it a better place. But the opposite can be true. We can misuse our gift and bring violence or destruction.

A mature and healthy sexuality is creative and transformative. Let's say you are a young man full of ambition, nursing your share of selfishness. You are attracted to a young woman; perhaps having sex is on your mind. But then you fall in love and the inner dynamics of sexuality help mature your desire.

You may still want sex, but intimacy and commitment come into play. You marry and for a time this suffices. Then you and your wife may begin to long for children; desire itself fuels this. They are born and you are swept up into a sort of loving you never imagined. Your children change your entire outlook on life. Whole new dimensions of desire are triggered so that you put your own needs aside to nurture and provide for your children. At each stage of your children's lives, you are pried open wider; their successes and failures challenge you at each stage. Slowly, imperceptibly, through the years you may find yourself becoming more unselfish and wise. Desire, working through us, if followed faithfully, takes us into a gracious adulthood.

If we commit ourselves to the long-term dynamics of our love, letting our initial attraction to each other flower, we discover that we are changed. On the most obvious, but also essential level, our sexuality, expressed in the act of making love with another person, is life giving. Together, we are capable of bringing a new life into the world. This is not merely a biological fact, but a spiritual one. Our children gift us and so do our spouses.

When a couple accepts the invitation to grow into love's fullness together, they can be sanctified, made holy. This is not an abstract, unworldly holiness, but a holiness born out of life's frustrations, delights, sorrows, and deep joys. We learn the real life lessons of love: over the dinner table, at the hospital bedside, in mutual care and self-giving, in cultivating respect for the otherness of the other and being willing to risk being made new in the crucible of intimacy.

It is not only with our families that we experience the creative, life-giving power of sexuality. Our friendships can be transformative as well. For a genuine and mature friendship (not simply a co-worker or an acquaintance) is a relationship of love, a mutual and equal love, which should have the highest good, and growth of both friends at its core. A true friend celebrates our victories, is a support in trouble, calls us to our best selves, and challenges us when we betray our deepest dreaming. Friendship in God is a great gift and its cultivation can be truly creative, bringing us into a fullness of personhood we could not have imagined.

**Channeling Our Creative Energy.** Until now we have spoken of the creative power of connecting, of the spiritual growth possible in loving relationships. We should also be aware that the deep desire to connect is one that will never be completely satisfied this side of heaven. Our sexuality is part of the divine fire. So we must learn to temper the fire with a spirit of chastity. Chastity is not the same thing as celibacy; it does not mean not marrying. Nor does it imply prudishness. To be chaste is to experience people, places, things, entertainment, and sex in a way that does not violate them or us. To be chaste is to experience people and things reverently, with respect.

There are many ways our sexuality, with its limitless energy, can be channeled. It may bring life in the context of healthy relationships. Or it may express itself in a profound solidarity with those who are poor or marginalized. It may take the form of a creative solitude in which we cultivate intimacy with God. It may flower in works of art, in music, song, dance, or in creative endeavors of all kinds. We speak of it as being generative.

Our companion for this session, Sr. Thea, never married or had children, yet she was a woman of radiance, whose sexuality was profoundly creative. Sexuality has to do with that part of us that longs for reconnection. In Sr. Thea's case, this desire expressed itself in her transformative work of breaking down the barriers of race prejudice. She believed people could know their common identity as children of God and rejoice in the One who loved them all into life. Her lyrical singing and her capacity for life flowed unbounded from her, captivating her listeners and bringing them closer to the God of joy.

## Sharing Our Faith

✠ Reflect on the relationships in your life—friends, spouses, family members—that have been life-giving. Share some ways in which they have been so.

✠ How might I be more reverent (chaste) in my relationships? Share ways in which your sexuality/your masculinity/your femininity has been life-giving to others. In what ways can I be more life-giving?

✠ Our sexuality is more than a physical passion. Sexuality is our passion for life. In what other ways, outside my relationships, could I express my creative capacities? How will I do so? Have I artistic gifts? Organizational skills? Community organizing skills?

## Living the Good News

*Choose how you feel the Word of God and your sharing challenge you to action for the week ahead. The best actions are always the ones that emerge from the specific contexts of your own lives and sharing. These suggested actions are just that, suggestions. If they capture your imagination and seem like the right action for your group or yourself, then proceed with one of them. If they do not, devise more appropriate individual and/or group actions.*

🌐 If you are married, commit to a Marriage Encounter Weekend with your spouse. If you are engaged, participate in an Engaged Encounter with your fiancé(e).

🌐 Act on ways through which your children or grandchildren and other young people you know may gain a healthy attitude toward sexuality.

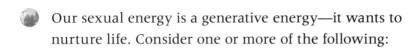 Our sexual energy is a generative energy—it wants to nurture life. Consider one or more of the following:

* Determine to spend time creatively with your children, grandchildren, nieces, nephews, etc., or youth in your parish, at school, or in your community.
* Volunteer to teach religious education classes.
* Share your faith journey with young people in a confirmation program.
* Volunteer to visit hospitalized children.
* Go with or organize a youth volunteer service trip in your community.
* Join a Big Brothers or Sisters program.

If you have musical or artistic skills, find out how you can use them to bring life to others. Join the choir, help decorate for the parish festival, start a quilting group, sew costumes for the parish school play. Use your imagination.

Facilitate younger people connecting with the elderly around the question of faith. Take a youth group to a retired sisters' community and interview those residents who are willing to talk about how their faith has sustained them for a lifetime. Or, arrange for your own children to spend time with a grandparent or elder who has lived a rich life of faith.

In your journal, record your reactions to several of the definitions of sexuality raised in this session.

Given where I am in my own life and as a response to the Word of God and our sharing, I feel called to

## Closing Prayer

*Share prayers of intercession, petition, or praise.*

*Close with Sr. Thea's words:*

> We come to prayer because God is our father,
> and God has promised us everlasting love,
> everlasting kindness and everlasting care....
> I'm somebody. I'm somebody special. I'm God's child.
> I can change things. I can make life better for myself,
> for my family, for my community, for my Church,
> for my world.
> I make life better when I care about somebody,
> when I reach out and touch somebody,
> when I smile, when I say yes to life and to laughter
> and to love and to hope and to joy—
> even in the midst of troubles.
> I make life better when I say yes to God's will
> as it manifests itself in the circumstances of my life.
> And I want to say yes to God.
> I want to say yes to life, yes to hope,
> yes to love, yes to you, yes to eternity.
> Amen.

## Looking Ahead

*Prepare at home for your next session by prayerfully reading and studying Session 11.*

## Informal Gathering

## SUGGESTIONS FOR FURTHER READING

John W. Crossin, *Friendship: The Key to Spiritual Growth,*
Paulist Press

Karol Wojtyla, *Love and Responsibility,*
Ignatius Press

*Sister Thea Bowman, Shooting Star:*
*Selected Writings and Speeches,* Edited by Celestine Cepress
St. Mary's Press

Richard R. Galliardetz, *A Daring Promise:*
*A Spirituality of Christian Marriage,*
The Crossroad Publishing Company

*United States Catholic Catechism for Adults:*
Chapter 30. The Sixth Commandment: Marital Fidelity;
Chapter 33. The Ninth Commandment: Practice Purity
of Heart

*Catechism of the Catholic Church:*
Paragraphs 2231-2350, 2360-2363

# Living the Life

## Sharing

*Briefly share on one of the following questions:*

"How am I right now?" or
"What good news would I like to share?"

## Sharing the Good News

*Share how you did with your action response from the last session (Living the Good News) or how you were able to incorporate the message of the last session into your daily lives.*

## Lifting Our Hearts ...

### ... in Song

*Play or sing one of the following or another song of your choice:*

"Here I Am Lord"
"Seek Ye First"

### ... in the Quiet

*Pause for a few moments of silence and enter more deeply into the presence of God.*

## ... in the Word

*Read aloud* Luke 15:11-32.

*Take a few minutes to ponder a word, a phrase, a question, or a feeling that rises up in you. Reflect on this quietly; then share it aloud.*

*(Even if no one wishes to reflect aloud, permit sufficient time for silent reflection.)*

## ... in Prayer

*Conclude with this prayer spoken together:*

> God of our days and our evenings,
> our summer and winter times,
> our hearts are made for you in every season.
> Yet much of the time they are fixed
> on anything else but you.
> May we learn to listen to your Word,
> hold it in our hearts and
> allow what we hear to guide and shape our lives.
> Amen.

## Our Companion on the Journey

# Dorothy Day

> "I shall meditate as I have been accustomed, in the
> little Italian church on Twelfth Street, by the
> side of the open window, looking out at the
> plants growing on the roof,
> the sweet corn, the boxes of herbs, the geraniums
> in bright bloom,
> and I shall rest happy in the presence of Christ on
> the altar,

and then I shall come home and I shall write …
    and try to catch some of these things
that happen to bring me nearer to God, to catch
    them and put them down on paper.
And because I am a woman involved
    in practical cares,
I cannot give the first half of the day to these
    things, but must meditate when I can,
early in the morning and on the fly during the day.
Not in the privacy of a study—but here, there and
    everywhere—
at the kitchen table, on the train, on the ferry,
    on my way to and from appointments,
and even while making supper or putting Teresa
    [Tamar] to bed."

Dorothy Day (20th century, America)

Dorothy Day is best known as the founder of the Catholic Worker movement. A life of intense seeking lay behind that foundation. Raised in an only nominally religious home, Dorothy first sought to make her mark as a journalist. Moved by the plight of the urban worker, she advocated for them with her socialist journalist friends. Eventually, the God-question began to dominate her life. Several failed relationships and the birth of a daughter led Dorothy to the doorstep of the Catholic Church. It was her collaboration with Peter Maurin, a French vagabond Catholic philosopher, which enabled her to bring together her faith and her concern for the poor. Her life was intensely busy and she chose to live with the "Christs of the breadline" and share their financial insecurity. Yet Dorothy's daily life and work were shaped by her reading of Scripture and saturated with the spirit of her faithful liturgical practice. Today the Catholic Worker movement continues her legacy by taking seriously the vision of the last judgment in Matthew 25 as it seeks to practice the corporal works of mercy in its Houses of Hospitality and by heeding the Sermon on the Mount in its advocacy of Christian pacifism.

## Encountering Wisdom for Life

THE SPIRIT-LED LIFE is something we all long for: it is what our hearts are made for. But too often we tend to think: "If I just follow all the rules," or "If I just get the doctrines straight," I will have this Christian thing down pat. But knowledge alone cannot save us. Simply knowing something, even something as primary as the central teachings of faith, is not enough to sustain us. "Pope John Paul II gave us a wonderful work in which the faith of centuries is explained synthetically: the *Catechism of the Catholic Church*.... Obviously, books alone are not enough. Form communities based on faith!" (Pope Benedict XVI, World Youth Day, August 21 2005, Cologne, Marienfield, Germany).

The Christian life is something we live, not merely a set of ideas. Truth is also a question of the heart. The task then for us in this session is to reflect on the questions: How do I develop the heart? What practices and exercises can allow me to grow in my love of God and others? What can I do to sustain myself over the long haul?

Tradition tells us that to grow in love we need to *practice* loving. We practice loving God through engaging regularly in prayer both private and communal. We practice loving one another by means of the works of mercy and active engagement with others. Finally, we continue to make ourselves vulnerable and able to love more generously (this means loving both friends and enemies) through forgiveness and reconciliation. What might these practices of love mean for us today, each in our own circumstance?

**First, practice personal prayer.** Prayer is about cultivating a relationship with God. If you pay attention to the Gospels you will notice that Jesus has an intense relationship with God. He teaches his followers a prayer (an incredibly powerful and crucial one) and also invites them by his parables and statements to form a living relationship with God. Dorothy Day disciplined herself to give time to prayer in the early hours of the morning, participated in daily Eucharist as the heart of her prayer, then simply raised her heart to God during the day. We may completely follow Dorothy's example. We may sit in silence and simply listen for the heartbeat of God. We may use traditional prayers or simply talk to God in our own ways.

Here is one suggestion that is time-tested and practiced by generations of the faithful in prayer.

### PRACTICING PERSONAL PRAYER

✦ ✦ ✦

Start with a passage from Scripture. A good suggestion is to select the reading of the day (you can find the reading of the day at www.usccb.org/nab/ or www.sacredspace.ie/). This way you will be praying with the rest of the Church and allowing your own very personal reflections to be gathered into the greater prayer that rises up from the heart of the community to God.

Read the passage aloud slowly. On one level you are reading for information—what is the point of the story? The gist of the passage? You might spend a few minutes reflecting on these questions. Maybe you have a Bible with commentary and you might want to read the notes that explain the passage's historical or theological import. But on another level you are reading not simply for information but in order to be formed, to be changed by the power of the Word.

So after you have read the passage aloud slowly go back and read it again with the sense that the passage is not just about the past but that it is speaking to *you right now*. This time stop if you find a word or a phrase that speaks to your heart. Perhaps you will be moved. Perhaps you will be comforted. Perhaps you will be struck by or challenged with something you've never considered before.

Then speak to God about what is in your heart. Do this simply, knowing God longs to be in communion with us and to have us communicate in return. Finally, you may simply want to hold what you have prayed or felt in your heart very quietly.

This practice, known as *lectio divina* or sacred reading, is one way we can deepen our love for God who loves us so and longs to have that love returned. Sacred reading is more than Bible study; it is like an extended conversation with a lover or a cherished friend. Sometimes we exchange information, but more often we share together the longings of our hearts, are challenged and comforted, confirmed and enlivened by one another. Finally, we simply enjoy each other's presence; we sit quietly side by side or we rest in each other's arms knowing we are loved beyond the words we exchange.

✛ ✛ ✛

**Second, engage in communal prayer.** Fr. Rolheiser states this principle boldly: in every circumstance of life, gather ritually in prayer. Why, you might ask, should I bother to get together with other people if I have a rich prayer life with God alone? The answer is simple. The Christian life is not a private undertaking meant for me alone. It is about being the Body of Christ in the world. Jesus promised that whenever a group of people gathers in prayer, he would be there with them. The Christian life is a life we sustain together. Unfortunately, ritual is something that, for the most part, we no longer understand. We tend to be ritually tone-deaf. But to be human is to be a creature hard wired for ritual.

This was evident in the spontaneous shrines that cropped up all over New York after 9/11. It is evident in the proliferation of men's ritual groups, of Alcoholics Anonymous meetings, or in the popularity of Native American sweat lodges. It is evident in liturgical dance, in choral or folk groups. Good ritual carries us beyond what we can rationally explain. It can bring about group unity, healing, and other kinds of transformation. It is there we acknowledge that our little lives are surrounded by a greater life. It is there we offer the worship for which our hearts are fitted.

Of course, as Catholics we have our Christ-centered sacramental tradition—our powerful rituals of baptism, confirmation, Eucharist, and so forth, in which we experience God's mediated action through symbols of water, oil, bread, wine. These are not just obligatory rites but containing and sustaining vessels, which not only keep us coming together but also keep us from falling apart. For over two thousand years the community that follows Jesus has been nurtured and sustained by ritually breaking open and sharing the Word of God and the bread of life.

The sustaining power of ritual is clear in Dorothy Day's life. She worked for decades in the most demanding conditions. When the homeless flocked to Catholic Worker Houses of

Hospitality, they brought the searing pain of broken lives. The dilapidated buildings in which the community lived were always in need of repair; food and money were always scarce; helpers came and went; problems were everywhere. Yet, daily liturgical prayer was at the heart of the community and Mass was always celebrated. It was there, in the deep ritual reservoir of faith, that Dorothy and her workers sustained themselves, reminded themselves of why they were doing what they were doing, and were nourished and strengthened to do the work they felt God called them to do.

**Third, love one another by practicing the works of mercy.** The corporal works of mercy are to feed the hungry; to give drink to the thirsty; to clothe the naked; to shelter the homeless; to visit the sick; to comfort those imprisoned; to bury the dead. The spiritual works of mercy are to instruct the uninformed; to counsel the doubtful; to admonish sinners; to bear wrongs patiently; to forgive offenses willingly; to comfort the afflicted; to pray for the living and the dead.

We have already seen in Session 8 how central the work of justice is to our faith. We referred then to the story of Fr. Damien of Molokai and his Hawaiian lepers. The practice of loving one another, whether it is expressed in dramatic ways, as with Fr. Damien or with Dorothy Day, is not only about "helping those in need," it is about learning to love as we have been loved. It changes and sustains us for the long haul.

**Fourth, love one another through practicing forgiveness and reconciliation.** Several years before he died, Henri Nouwen, one of the great spiritual writers of the 20th century, wrote a book entitled *The Return of the Prodigal Son*, which is both a commentary on a painting by Rembrandt and a reflection on God as loving parent. It concerns the scripture story with which we began this session. Nouwen points out that in Rembrandt's picture the figure of the father, which represents God, has several features. His eyes are shut: he sees the prodigal son not with his eyes but with his heart. Moreover, the God-figure has one male hand, which pulls the wayward son to himself, and one female hand, which caresses the son's back. This God offers love that is both constant and compassionate. We can see ourselves in the figures of the wayward son and the bitter older brother, but what we are also invited to see and identify with is the Father as all-embracing, all-forgiving, caressing compassion.

Ultimately, we, too, are meant to radiate this same sort of love. To do that, we need the courage to let ourselves be embraced by God when we are sinful and bitter. We need a radical honesty with ourselves, an honesty that has nothing to do with putting ourselves down. We are human and we sin. We sometimes fail to repent, to accept God's mercy. In so doing, we reject the forgiveness of our sins and the salvation offered by the Holy Spirit.

We are too often like the older son who cannot see his own self-righteousness and his incapacity to forgive as his father can. Like the wayward son, being honest about our weaknesses frees us to accept the gratuitous forgiveness offered us by God. In our turn, we are asked to forgive and to seek reconciliation with one another.

We are to practice loving as we are loved by God. Forgiveness is not simple nor is it ignoring when wrong has been done. But vengeance or hard-heartedness and resentment or refusing to seek reconciliation are not the practices of God that Jesus gives us. We can extend this love (loving as God has loved us) to others to the extent that we have had the honest courage to let ourselves be forgiven and embraced when we have failed.

When we can be open to God's loving embrace, we free ourselves to live more fully in harmony with our Christian vocation. In trying to sustain ourselves as Christians, few things are as important as worshiping the right God, the God whom Jesus reveals. It is all too easy to make gods of our own personal, political, or national agendas. Fr. Rolheiser challenges us to take the first commandment seriously: "You shall have no other gods before me." In addition to not having false gods, we need to have a realistic image of who God is.

What is your image of God? Fr. Rolheiser puts it this way: in some circles, God's primary facial expression is a frown. He is looking at the world and seeing there a confused, morally lax, and sexually promiscuous rabble. His first reaction to us is always displeasure. This is a god who is a projection of our own anger and incapacity to forgive each other. In other circles, God is different, but no closer to what is prescribed in the first commandment. This is an anxious, worried, hypersensitive, politically correct, workaholic, and whining god. This god also wears a frown and disapproves of the world's stupidity and lack of social conscience.

God, whom Jesus calls Father, does not see the world with a frown. God, who made the world, declared it good. In God's infinite mercy, that original glance of blessing has not changed, despite the existence of evil and sin. God's smile was and is upon us. Awareness of God's smile was very much a part of Jesus' consciousness. At his baptism in the Jordan, God, his Father, proclaimed, "You are my Beloved, my blessed one, my Son, in whom I am pleased." When Jesus looks on others, he sees them with this sense of blessing. So, too, are we beloved sons and daughters, called to see the world and each other with eyes of love. This is the God we, as Christians, worship. It was the vision of such a reconciling God that underlay Dorothy Day's Christian life-long pacifism.

These four practices of loving—personal prayer, communal prayer, the works of mercy, and forgiving others as we have been forgiven—are what will sustain us in the day-to-day practice of faith. Faith is not simply a set of ideas or the observance of a moral code; it is a life practice whose way is opened for us by Jesus, who taught us that God seeks us out in the silence of our own hearts, when we gather together, and when we love one another as we have been loved.

## Sharing Our Faith

✛ What sort of *personal* prayer has sustained me over the years? Share those ways you have nurtured your personal relationship with God. If you have felt the lack of personal prayer, discuss with your group your struggle to pray or your desire to pray more deeply. Remember, prayer can happen in many ways.

✛ Tell of a time you witnessed or performed a corporal or spiritual work of mercy or tell of a forgiveness story in your life.

✛ Reflect on Dorothy Day's spirituality of living with the "Christs of the breadline." How can I live out my belief in what it means to be the Body of Christ?

## Living the Good News

*Choose how you feel the Word of God and your sharing challenge you to action for the week ahead. The best actions are always the ones that emerge from the specific contexts of your own lives and sharing. These suggested actions are just that, suggestions. If they capture your imagination and seem like the right action for your group or yourself, then proceed with one of them. If they do not, devise more appropriate individual and/or group actions.*

🌐 Resolve specific ways personal prayer will play a greater part in your life.

In silence, read again the story of the Prodigal Son. Then bring your honest self before God, with all your gifts and failures. With whom in the story do you identify? Spend time quietly letting the story speak to you. You might want to use the process of *lectio divina* to guide your reflection (see pp. 133-34). Record your reflections in a journal or share your reflection, as it seems appropriate.

As a group, attend a communal worship service you do not usually attend in order to expand your sense of praying with the larger Church. This could be a service of morning prayer, vespers, daily Mass, or a devotional service (the Rosary, First Friday Holy Hour, adoration, a Marian devotion, Benediction, etc.)

Consider the broken relationships in your life. In what ways might you begin the process of forgiveness and healing? Act on your reflections. If you find yourself dealing with questions of serious abuse or violence, seek the counsel of your priest or pastoral minister before beginning the work of forgiveness.

Celebrate the sacrament of reconciliation.

Choose one of the traditional works of spiritual and corporal mercy and practice it this week. Journal about your growth.

Given where I am in my own life and as a response to the Word of God and our sharing, I feel called to

## Closing Prayer

*Share prayers of intercession, petition, or praise.*

## Looking Ahead

*Prepare at home for your next session by prayerfully reading and studying Session 12.*

## Informal Gathering

## Suggestions for Further Reading

*What Makes Us Catholic: Eight Gifts for Life,* Thomas H. Groome,
HarperCollins

*Virtues for Ordinary Christians,* James F. Keenan,
Sheed & Ward

*The Catholic Prayer Book,* Tony Castle, II, Michael Buckley, S.J.,
Charis Books

Dorothy Day, *The Long Loneliness,* HarperSanFrancisco
(trademark of HarperCollins Publishers Inc.) or
*Loaves and Fishes,* Orbis Books

*Dorothy Day: Selected Writings,* Edited by Robert Ellsberg,
Orbis Books

Henri Nouwen, *The Return of the Prodigal Son,* Doubleday

Benedict J. Groeschel, C.F.R., *Questions and Answers About
Your Journey to God,* Our Sunday Visitor

*United States Catholic Catechism for Adults:*
Chapter 35. God Calls Us to Pray;
Chapter 36. Jesus Taught Us to Pray;
Chapter 18. Sacrament of Penance and Reconciliation:

*Catechism of the Catholic Church:*
Prayer:
Paragraphs 2559-2565, 2627-2647, 2697-2745
Works of Mercy:
Paragraphs 2443-2448
Forgiveness and Reconciliation:
Paragraphs 2631, 2838-2845
Sacrament of Penance and Reconciliation:
Paragraphs 1422-1498

# Being a Mystic in Everyday Life

## Finding God in All Things

## Sharing

*Briefly share on one of the following questions:*

"How am I right now?" or
"What good news would I like to share?"

## Sharing the Good News

*Share how you did with your action response from the last session (Living the Good News) or how you were able to incorporate the message of the last session into your daily lives.*

## Lifting Our Hearts ...

### ... in Song

*Play or sing one of the following or another song of your choice:*

"River of Glory"
"How Great Thou Art"

### ... in the Quiet

*Pause for a few moments of silence and enter more deeply into the presence of God.*

### ... in the Word

*Read aloud* Psalm 139:1-18.

*Take a few minutes to ponder a word, a phrase, a question, or a feeling that rises up in you. Reflect on this quietly; then share it aloud.*

*(Even if no one wishes to reflect aloud, permit sufficient time for silent reflection.)*

### ... in Prayer

*Conclude with this prayer spoken together:*

> Lord of all our days,
> of our beginnings and endings,
> of our days of boredom and weariness
> and our days of sunlit joy,
> teach us to see you in all and everything.
> Open our eyes and our hearts
> to your ever-present presence.
> Amen.

## Our Companion on the Journey

# Father Karl Rahner, S.J.

"I should like to bring my daily drudge before you, O Lord
—the long hours and days crammed
with everything else but you.
Look at this daily drudge, my gentle God,
you who are merciful to us men and women
for whom daily drudge is virtually all we are ...
Is there a route through the drudge to you?
... where are you to be found,
if the enjoyment of the everyday makes us forget you,

and if the disappointments of the everyday
have not yet found you?
... if there is nowhere where you have given me a place
to which we can just flee away in order to find you,
and if everything can be the loss of you, the One,
then I must also be able to find you in everything ...
I can only stammer a request for your
most commonplace of gifts,
which is also your greatest: the gift of your love.
Let me, as I grasp after the things of this world in joy or pain,
grasp and love *you* through them...."

Karl Rahner (20th century, Germany/Austria)

KARL RAHNER of the Society of Jesus is known as one of the modern world's most notable Catholic theologians. His role as a theological advisor during the Second Vatican Council, his voluminous publications, his involvement in international theological debate, and his impact on students who attended his classes at universities in Innsbruck, Munich, and Munster, all contributed to his influence on theology. But Karl Rahner was not only a man of noble thoughts. His probing mind was paired with an equally probing heart. Trained in the Ignatian tradition of spirituality as a Jesuit, Rahner was taught to "find God in all things," to search for the presence of God in the fabric of ordinary life. Jesuits have often been called "contemplatives in action" and Rahner is an example of this claim. The experience of prayer and a deeply mystical faith animated his theology. For him, mysticism—the direct experience of God—is not an esoteric occurrence reserved for a few, but an experience at the heart of faith itself. He believed that the experience of God, in which God is present in consciousness—not just as a thought or a spoken word but also as a living reality—is the inheritance of all Christians.

## Encountering Wisdom for Life

IN OUR LAST SESSION we explored some of the ways in which we are sustained in the life of faith. We considered a few of the practices that can establish the habit of faithfulness. In this session we will continue our practice of faith, but in a different way. More fundamental than all the religious activities we do, the prayers we say, the devotional gestures we make, is our capacity for God. We are all called to be mystics of the everyday. This may seem like an extravagant claim, but it is only if we misunderstand the term "mystic."

Mystic does not refer to someone who has paranormal experiences: ecstasies, levitations, visions, or locutions. No. What is meant by being a mystic of the everyday is being able to recover the ancient instinct for astonishment. It means we have recovered the capacity to be touched by God in a way that goes beyond what we think, express, imagine, or even clearly feel. Mystical knowledge is real knowledge, but it is experienced, to use St. Paul's words, "in a mirror, dimly" (1 Corinthians 13:12).

**Practicing the Presence of God.** Let's back up a little here and begin with the idea that many of us are agnostics (we doubt there is a God; or if we have no doubt, perhaps we are functional agnostics, living as though we do not believe in the power of God to take us beyond our limits and fears). "What," you say, "not I!" But today, even among pious churchgoers, there is functional unbelief. We may be able to recite the Creed and refer to the *Catechism,* but God is not experienced as alive, a person to whom we can relate as friend, lover, companion, and comforter. Instead, God is experienced as a religion, a church, a moral philosophy, a guide for private virtue, an imperative for justice, or as a nostalgia for things "as they used to or should be."

God as a living person is absent from our ordinary consciousness. However, God is, in fact, always present, but we are not always present to God. Jesus says, "Blessed are the pure in heart: they shall see God." Awareness of God, this suggests, is attached to a state of awareness that is known as purity of heart. Classic spiritual writers have identified this state—the ongoing practice of purifying consciousness so as to better experience God—as a contemplative one.

To be contemplative is to be fully awake to all the dimensions within ordinary experience. If our ordinary awareness is not distorted by excessive narcissism, pragmatism, and restlessness (those challenges of our culture that we dealt with in Session 2), there will be present to us, alongside everything else that makes up experience, a sense of the sacred, the infinite, God. Brother Lawrence of the Resurrection, a 17th century Carmelite brother who spent his life working among the pots and pans of the monastery kitchen, gave a name to what we are talking about. He called it "the practice of the presence of God." He was certain that anyone could cultivate this sort of purity of heart. And a lot of folks from outside the monastery came to learn from him.

That is also what Karl Rahner's prayer (see pp. 145-46) is about. It is a prayer for the grace to experience God, however darkly, in all and everything. Cultivating a contemplative spirit is something that takes place over a lifetime and cannot be reduced to a few principles. Nevertheless, we can suggest some starting points here. It will be especially important to cultivate practices, such as those described in the Living the Good News section or others like them, over a period of time.

**Cultivate a Sense of Wonder.** First, a contemplative spirit requires the recovery or cultivation of a sense of wonder. A genuine contemplative awareness requires that we let go of some of the ways we have become accustomed to getting along up to this point.

✳ We will have to rely less on having our immediate whims and self-referential desires met. A life awash in indulgence, seeking to get whatever we want, whenever we want it is a life that has no room for wonder, for being surprised by the small graces that punctuate our days. If we always relate to others as potential rivals, sex objects, or enemies, we are seeing them only as they relate to our own perceived self-interest. Our awareness is narrow and fear-driven. We will need to let go of our self-protective fears and prejudices. We will need to allow ourselves to be remade by God, to be opened in trust and in the capacity to love.

✳ In addition, we will also have to be less pragmatic than we are used to being. We are all about getting the job done, checking things off the list, and attending to the bottom line. We will have to let ourselves be less driven, to be willing to stop and appreciate what we have. We will have to be willing to attend to a needy friend whether or not the laundry needs to be done, or plant a spring garden for the sheer joy of it, or spend the day playing with our children, whether or not we are frantic to rise to the top of our profession. Our awareness must be expanded by letting go of our pragmatism.

✳ Finally, we will have to get used to letting go of all of our false securities. We are used to feeling safe by relying mainly on conceptual knowledge. We are used to feeling safe by accumulating possessions. We are used to having our lives dominated by the need to feel secure, whether it is through having a lot of things or surrounding ourselves with locks and gates and weapons. We need to learn a new purity of awareness, one that can come at the world with more trust and openness. None of this is to suggest that normal prudence is not a good thing. But to the extent we need to always be right, to have a pat answer, to believe there is only one way to see the world, to the extent we see the world through eyes of fear and self-protection, we cannot see with a contemplative eye. The glories of God's world, the astonishing beauty of God's creatures, the mystery of God's deep grace working in human hearts, the drama of our struggles to live fully, to strain against our failures, rejoice in our redemptions, and carry one another home: *all this is charged with divine presence.* We need to purify our awareness in order to receive what there is in wonder.

**Learn to Ponder.** Second, a contemplative spirit requires that we need to learn to ponder. What does this mean? The reference here is the scriptural witness of the Virgin Mary who pondered these things in her heart (Luke 2:19). To ponder something is less a question of intellectually considering it as it is of holding it inside one's self, complete with all the tension that brings. To ponder something means to be willing to live with paradox in a creative way. To ponder means to stand before life's great mysteries, as did Mary at the moment of the Annunciation and at the foot of the cross. To refuse to expand the heart enough to hold all these contradictions is to abort the deep wisdom that can be gained as we ponder.

Jesus, of course, is the most powerful example of this process. He was on the receiving end of hatred, jealousy, and anger, but he never passed these on to others. Instead he carried these and held them together in his heart with an unfathomable love until they were transformed into forgiveness, compassion, and love.

Jacques Maritain, a Catholic philosopher, once stated that a great spiritual tragedy of our day is that many people of good will could become persons of noble soul if only they would not panic and resolve the painful tensions within their lives too prematurely, but rather stay with them long enough until those tensions are transformed and give birth to what is most noble inside us—compassion, forgiveness, and love.

The recovery of a sense of wonder and the cultivation of the ability to ponder things in the heart—these are needed to be a mystic of the everyday. These are what are needed for the spiritual renewal of our world.

## Sharing Our Faith

✠ What do I see as the difference among these three kinds of prayer:
> reciting a prayer
> talking with God
> listening to God?

✠ How can I develop a greater sense of wonder?

✠ Are there any words or images from Psalm 139 that touched your heart? Share how these spoke to you.

✠ Would I say I am engaged in finding God in every way and everything? If not, what are some ways I can cultivate a way of finding God in all things?

## Living the Good News

*Choose how you feel the Word of God and your sharing challenge you to action for the week ahead. The best actions are always the ones that emerge from the specific contexts of your own lives and sharing. These suggested actions are just that, suggestions. If they capture your imagination and seem like the right action for your group or yourself, then proceed with one of them. If they do not, devise more appropriate individual and/or group actions.*

 Make it a habit to "review your day" at the end of each day. You may simply do this as a mental exercise or you may record your reflections in a journal. Ignatius of Loyola, founder of the Jesuits, recommended a spiritual exercise he called the examination of conscience. Jesuits today are more likely to refer to it as the examen of consciousness. For our purposes we might simply name it the Review of Your Day. Take several minutes in a quiet setting to look back prayerfully at the events of the day. Be attentive to the ways in which God was present to you, even if you might not have been overly aware of it at the time. A visit from a dear friend, the kindness of a stranger, an experience of forgiveness, a glimpse of an exquisite sunset, a tender or exhilarating moment with a family member, a consoling moment of prayer, the joy of a garden, an inspiring story of courage, the beauty of a song, meeting a challenge, accomplishing a difficult but meaningful task, learning a lesson in faith: all these and a thousand other moments in a day can be gathered up and offered to God in thanksgiving. Review as well the times during the day when you were too busy or distracted to attend to God's presence. Offer these to God as well, knowing God's mercy is abundant.

In summary:

Make it a habit to "review your day" every evening.

Prayerfully look over the events of your day (visits, calls, strangers, nature, ordinary tasks, surprises, distractions).

How was God present in that?

Offer the day's events up to God.

Give thanks and ask forgiveness.

Practice being attentive to the here and now. Take a solitary walk in a reasonably quiet place, in your neighborhood, a park, a natural setting, a public recreational walkway. If this is not possible because of the weather or your circumstances, choose a quiet place and time in your own home (before others are awake or after they are asleep or have left the house, in a place where you will not be distracted by TV, radio, or phone) or at or near your place of work (a chapel, a park bench, a quiet room). While you are walking or simply sitting, give your full attention to what is around you. Feel the breeze, hear the sounds, be aware of the movement or relaxation of your body, note the colors, textures, and sights. Feel that sense of wonder! Try to stay present. If you find yourself thinking about tonight's dinner or yesterday's conversation or your to-do list, gently bring yourself back to where you are and what you are doing: simply being present to the moment God gives you. Let yourself breathe in the present moment with gratitude.

IN SUMMARY:

Be attentive to the here and now.

Take a solitary walk or find a quiet place to reflect.

Give your full attention to what is around you.

Stay present to the experience (if distractions enter draw yourself back).

Breathe in the present moment with gratitude.

Reflect alone or with others on four scripture passages: Luke 1:26-38 (the Annunciation), Luke 2:15-20 (the visit of the shepherds), Luke 2:22-35 (the Presentation), and John 19:25-27 (at the foot of the cross). Using Mary as a companion, consider what it might mean to have a heart that can ponder and hold together enormous tension creatively.

"Kiss the Leper" The title of this exercise is suggested by St. Francis of Assisi, who discovered that in touching the poorest of the poor he touched Christ. Today, God can also be revealed to us in those who are otherwise forgotten in our competitive, success-oriented world. The lepers of our day have many faces: those who are aged, sick, dying, impoverished, handicapped, lonely, displaced, refugees, etc. Arrange to volunteer at a homeless shelter, the Special Olympics, a hospital, a nursing home, hospice, or refugee agency. Realize while you may be helping others, they are also helping you. You are also encountering Christ on the cross in those who are marginalized. Arrange to meet after your volunteer time to share your reflections with others. Be frank about any discomfort or prejudices you might feel. Take these to God in prayer and ask St. Francis to be your companion.

Given where I am in my own life and as a response to the Word of God and our sharing, I feel called to

## Closing Prayer

*Share prayers of intercession, petition, or praise.*

*Then pray the following together:*

> Creator God,
> you are the Alpha and Omega,
> our source and cherished end.
> May we always seek you in everything:
> in our loves, our enemies, our fears, our joys.
> May your peace permeate our days,
> your wonder be ever before us.
> Amen.

## Looking Ahead

This is the final session of *Longing for the Holy,* but your personal and collective journey does not end here. The Christian life is just that, a life, not a study session, not simply a set of abstractions or rules. It is an ongoing process of growth and exploration. As you continue that exploration, may your lives be richly blessed and may you become more generous followers of Jesus the Christ.

Perhaps your group would like to continue meeting to pray together. **RENEW International offers faith-sharing material that will help you continue the journey.**

*WHY CATHOLIC? Journey through the Catechism* **Series**

> *The Profession of Faith: What We Believe*
> *The Celebration of the Christian Mystery: Sacraments*
> *Life in Christ: Walking with God*
> *Christian Prayer: Deepening My Experience of God*

*PrayerTime: Faith-Sharing Reflections on the Sunday Gospels,* Cycle A, B, C

**A sampling of our IMPACT Series**

*Finding God@Work: Practicing Spirituality in Your Workplace*
*At Prayer with Mary*
*Awakening the Mystic Within*
*Discipleship of Nonviolence*
*Grieving the Death of a Loved One*

Contact:

## RENEW International

1232 George Street
Plainfield, NJ 07062-1717

| | |
|---|---|
| Phones: | 908-769-5400 (inquiries) |
| | 888-433-3221 (orders only) |
| Fax: | 908-769-5660 |
| Website: | www.renewintl.org |
| Email: | resources@renewintl.org |

## Informal Gathering

## SUGGESTIONS FOR FURTHER READING

Ronald Rolheiser O.M.I., *The Shattered Lantern:*
*Rediscovering a Felt Presence of God,*
The Crossroad Publishing Company

Wendy M. Wright, *Seasons of a Family's Life:*
*Cultivating the Contemplative Spirit at Home,*
Jossey-Bass

Brother Lawrence, *The Practice of the Presence of God with*
*Spiritual Maxims: The Spiritual Secrets of a Humble Brother*
*Who Enjoyed Closeness with God,*
Revell

*Karl Rahner: Spiritual Writings,* Edited by Philip Endean, S.J.,
Modern Spiritual Masters Series,
Orbis Books

*Catechism of the Catholic Church:*
Paragraphs 208, 1148, 2144, 2655, 2709-2719

# Music Appendix

Songs are listed by title, author and/or composer, copyright holder or publisher; also indicated is an album on which to find the song.

\* Songs marked by an asterisk are on RENEW International's thirteen-song compilation CD: *Songs for Longing for the Holy.* You can get more information, and/or order this CD online, at www.renewintl.org

SESSION 1

\* "Gathered in the Love of Christ"
    Marty Haugen (GIA)
    Album: *The Song and the Silence*

"Your Love Is Finer than Life"
    Marty Haugen (GIA)
    Album: *Gather Us In*

SESSION 2

\* "Everyday God"
    Bernadette Farrell (OCP)
    Album: *Restless is the Heart*

"Hosea"
    Gregory Norbet
    (The Benedictine Foundation of the State of Vermont, Inc.)
    Album: *Listen*

# MUSIC APPENDIX

SESSION 3

* "Anthem" (We Are Called, We are Chosen)
  Tom Conry (OCP)
  Album: *Consecrated*

"I Have Loved You"
  Michael Joncas (OCP)
  Album: *On Eagle's Wings*

SESSION 4

* "Weave One Heart"
  [E Haku I Ka Pu'u Wai]
  Marty Haugen (GIA)
  Album: *Spirit of Malia*

"Jesus, the Lord"
  Robert F. O'Connor, SJ (OCP)
  Album: *Come to the Water*, Volume I

SESSION 5

* "I Am For You"
  Rory Cooney (GIA)
  Album: *Spirit of Malia*

"Lord, You Have Come" / "Pescador de Hombres"
  Cesáreo Gabaráin (OCP)
  Album: *Pescador de Hombres*

SESSION 6

* "Join in the Dance"
  Daniel L. Schutte (OCP)
  Album: *Glory in the Cross – Music for the Easter Triduum*

"Eye Has Not Seen"
  Marty Haugen (GIA)
  Album: *Anthology: 1980-1984*

# MUSIC APPENDIX

Session 7

* "For Living For Dying"
  Donna Peña (GIA)
  Album : *Spirit of Malia*

"Song of the Body of Christ" / "Canción del Cuerpo de Christo"
David Haas (GIA)
Album: *Spirit of Malia*

Session 8

* "We Come to Your Feast"
  Michael Joncas (GIA)
  Album: *Spirit of Malia*

"Pan de Vida"
Bob Hurd (GIA)
Album: *Pan de Vida*

Session 9

* "This Is (Song of Micah)"
  Liam Lawton (GIA)
  Album: *In the Quiet*

"We Are Called"
David Haas (GIA)
Album: *Blest Are They, the Best of David Haas, Volume 1*

Session 10

* "We Have Been Told"
  David Haas (GIA)
  Album: *You Are Mine: The Best of David Haas, Volume 2*

"You Are Mine"
David Haas (GIA)
Album: *You Are Mine, the Best of David Haas, Volume 2*

SESSION 11

\* "Here I am Lord"
    Michael Ward (World Library Publications)
    Album: *Sing My Soul* (Katy Feeney)

"Seek Ye First"
    Karen Lafferty (Maranatha Music)
    Album: *Country Worship – Seek Ye First*

SESSION 12

\* "River of Glory"
    © 1991 Daniel L. Schutte (OCP)
    Album: *Glory in the Cross-Music for the Easter Triduum*

"How Great Thou Art"
    Stuart K. Hine (OCP)
    Album: What Wondrous Love

\* "Heal Me, Lord"
    Cathy Riso (Olive Branch Publishing / Frankie's Farm Music)
    Album: *Renew the Face of the Earth Volume 2* (White Dove)

# Addresses of Publishers of Music Resources

## Katy Feeney Tapes
168 Cottage Avenue
Mt. Vernon, NY 10550
katyfeeney@aol.com

## GIA Publications, Inc.
7404 South Mason Avenue
Chicago, Il 60638
708-496-3800
www.giamusic.com

## OCP Publications
5536 NE Hassalo
Portland, OR 97213
800-548-8749
www.ocp.org

## RENEW International
1232 George Street
Plainfield, NJ 07081
Phone: 908-769-5400
Orders: 888-433-3221
Fax:    908-769-5660
Website: www.renewintl.org

## White Dove
23120 Lyons Ave
Suite 5-467
Santa Clarita, CA 91321
Phone: 520-219-3824
www.whitedoveproductions.com

# Acknowledgments

W<small>E GRATEFULLY ACKNOWLEDGE</small> the use of the following quotations:

The Scripture quotations contained herein are from the New Revised Standard Version Bible (containing the Old and New Testaments with the Apocryphal/Deuterocanonical Books), copyright © 1989 by the Division of Christian Education of the National Council of the Churches of Christ in the U.S.A., and are used by permission. All rights reserved.

Reasonable effort has been made to locate original sources. When not available, secondary sources are included. Where citations are not included, quotations are considered to be fair use of copyrighted work. The publisher appreciates information on original sources and will include them in subsequent printings.

p. 22, from *Francis de Sales, Jane de Chantal: Letters of Spiritual Direction* by Péronne Marie Thibert, Published by Paulist Press, 1988.

p. 32, from *Showings, Julian of Norwich,* Published by Paulist Press, 1978.

pp. 54-55, St. Teresa of Avila, from *The Essential Mystics* edited by Andrew Harvey. Published by Harper One, 1997.

p. 66, from *Elizabeth Ann Seton.* Published by Penguin Books, 1993.

p. 80, "Rules given by Don Bosco," from *Heart Speaks to Heart: the Salesian Tradition* by Wendy M. Wright. Published by Orbis Books, 2004.

pp. 88-89, from *I Sought and I Found:*
*My Experience of God and of the Church*, by Carlo Carretto.
Published by Orbis Books, 1984.

p. 92, from *Archbishop Romero: Memories and Reflections*
by Jon Sobrino. Published by Orbis Books:
Spiritual Masters Series, 1990.

p. 95, "I received the sacrament I still believe in ...,"
from *Essays by André Dubus.*
Published by Alfred Knopf, 1997.

p. 104, Quote from Bishop Maigret in *Holy Man:*
*Father Damien of Molokai* by Gaven Davis.
Published by University of Hawaii Press, 1973.

pp. 113-14, "The Lord's Prayer," from *The Holy Longing:*
*The Search for a Christian Spirituality*
by Ronald Rolheiser, copyright © 1998 by Ronald Rolheiser.
Used by permission of Doubleday,
a division of Random House, Inc.

pp. 118-19, "Formation in a New Age,"
quoted in *Sister Thea Bowman: Shooting Star,*
St. Mary's Press.

pp. 130-31, *The Long Loneliness: The Autobiography of Dorothy Day*
by Dorothy Day [illustrated by Fritz Eichenberg],
Harper & Row Publishers, 1952.

pp. 144-45, *Karl Rahner, Spiritual Writings* by Karl Rahner, S.J.,
edited and introduced by Philip Endean, S.J.
Published by Orbis Books, 2004.